*Be #ReMarkiTable in 2021*
*Marki Lemons Ryhal*

Please listen, subscribe, write a review, and share the Social Selling Made Simple podcast: ***http://www.socialsellingmadesimplepodcast.com.***

***Social Selling Made Simple*** is the place for entrepreneurs to learn how to use social media and technology so you can sell more and help more people

# The Social Selling Journal

*A 66-Day Guide to Creating the Habits to Achieve Your Business Social Goals*

**Marki Lemons Ryhal**

Email: info@markilemons.com
7300 S. Cottage Grove Ave.
Chicago, IL 60619

Copyright © 2020, ReMarkiTable, LLC

All rights reserved. No part of this book shall be reproduced, stored in a retrieval system, or transmitted by any means other than through ReMarkiTable, LLC without written permission from the publisher.

Published by ReMarkiTable, LLC
7300 S. Cottage Grove, Ave.,
Chicago, IL 60653
https://www.markilemons.com
Email: info@markilemons.com

First Printing: April 2020

Paperback ISBN: 978-1-7349828-0-0

eBook ISBN: 978-1-7349828-1-7

Place of Publication: Chicago, Illinois, USA

Paperback Library of Congress Number: 2020907543

**Trademarks**

All terms mentioned in this book that are known to be trademarks or service marks have been appropriately capitalized. Neither ReMarkiTable LLC, nor any of its imprints, can attest to the accuracy of this information. Use of a term in this book should not be regarded as affecting the validity of any trademark or service mark.

**Warning and Disclaimer**

Every effort has been made to make this journal as complete and as accurate as possible. The information provided is on an "as is" basis. The author(s), publisher, and their agents assume no responsibility for errors or omissions. Nor do they assume liability or responsibility to any person or entity with respect to any loss or damages arising from the use of information contained herein.

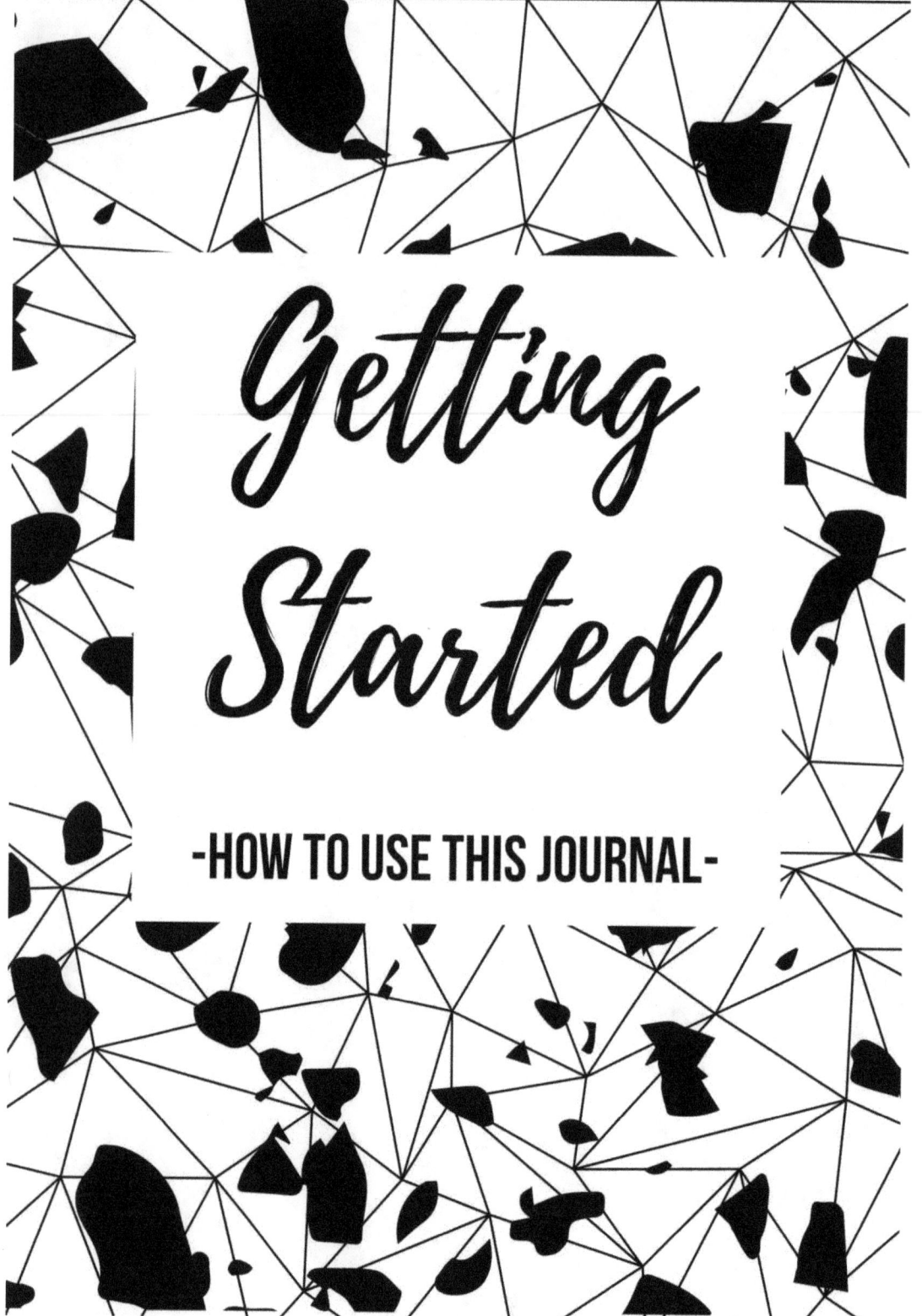

What is the Social Selling Journal?

The Social Selling Journal is all about being social every day, both online and offline, to stay number one in your customer's mind.

How does the Social Selling Journal work?

The Social Selling Journal is 66 days of social accountability. It takes exactly 66 days for a new behavior to become a habit. Step-by-step, the Social Selling Journal will guide you toward creating and sustaining new social behaviors in your life.

We start with three steps:

Step 1: Create your "SMART" goals (details on the next pages)

Step 2: Listen and Subscribe to www.socialsellingmadesimplepodcast.com

Step 3: Accomplish your goals!

Social media has forever changed how we conduct business. In 2006, no one ever imagined that Facebook would grow to over two billion monthly users!

Technology is always changing, and to survive in today's world of business, you must embrace the change and have a strategic plan in place to bridge your online and offline marketing.

While on maternity leave in 2007, I finally had a chance to Google my name. I was very disappointed that less than ten sources referenced me. As I was bringing a new life into the world, I decided to embark on a new marketing plan that would include social media marketing, social media tools, and gamification (terms I was unfamiliar with at the time). It took me over a year to make up my mind that I needed to get serious. Finally, in October 2008, I made up my mind and spent the rest of 2008, setting my social media plan in motion.

Along the way, I realized that the average person would be discouraged and would abandon their social media marketing plan because it was time-consuming and complicated. Therefore, I wrote a step-by-step guide as I implemented my new marketing plan so that others would have a road map that would save them energy, money, and time. The goal is for you to connect with customers where the customer is comfortable. Online is the new hot spot.

Let the connections begin!

1. **Set your goals.** Do you want to expand your brand, increase sales, establish yourself as a local authority, increase networking opportunities, or gain media exposure?
2. **Identify your customers:** Gen X, Gen Y, Baby Boomers, Millennials, or Gen Z.
3. **Research keywords using www.google.com/trends.** Research five terms that you will use to write your future social media marketing posts (and also add to your resume and bio). When researching keywords, you need to think like a consumer and search the way someone unfamiliar with your industry or business would search. In my line of business, we use terms and acronyms that no one would ever search, so using those terms in our marketing will not help with our search engine optimization (SEO).
4. **Write your social bio.** Your bio should include words that people search for when they want to purchase the products or services you offer. The length of your bio should be between 120-160 characters.
5. **Update your resume.**
6. **Select one professional photo to use.**
7. **Set up a Google Account**
   https://www.google.com/accounts/NewAccount:
    a. Gmail – works with an existing email address, compatible with Outlook, POP3, and IMAP supported and is smartphone-friendly.

a. Google Docs – spreadsheets, word processing, presentations, and forms.
   b. Google Sites – simple editable websites, choice of templates, and company intranets.
   c. Google Calendar – share your calendar with co-workers, embed on a website, collaborate with others, syncs with Outlook and iCal, and multiple calendars.
8. **Set-up an Excel template.** Log your username and passwords, or use a Google Spreadsheet.
9. **Purchase a domain name,** for your blog or website at www.godaddy.com.

1. Most of us want our businesses to grow but are unable to make it happen because of poor planning. The key to learning the art of proper goal-setting is to stop avoiding it! Seize the opportunity to set your own personal goals. Don't be ashamed to write them down, even if you feel they are just small goals that need not be written.
2. Know that there are no small goals. The fact that you set it as a goal in the first place means that it's relevant to you. Therefore, what is relevant is never small and is worth aspiring for.
3. Start to develop and set your goals. The best way to start good goal-setting is to write down your goals in order of importance. Explore more ways to effectively achieve each goal and force yourself to apply what you learned. Eventually, it will develop as a good habit. Stay committed for 66 days.
4. One effective strategy for creating realistic goals is to follow S.M.A.R.T. goal-setting. S.M.A.R.T. means :

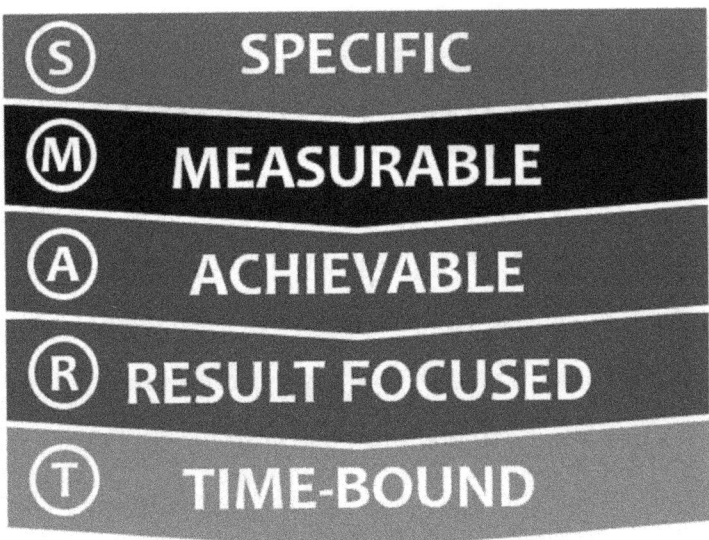

5. To summarize the idea for newbies, you have to start with small and uncomplicated goals. Write them down in your journal and make sure you have it handy. Set a realistic timeline for each goal and use this journal as a way to remind yourself to act on it every day.

I have heard many stories about people who failed because they did not believe in their goals. We are capable of achieving great things, but due to our scarcity mindset combined with a disbelieving heart, we fall short of our expectations.

Think with the end in mind! Your weekly goals are goals that will lead you to successfully completing your monthly goals. Your monthly goals will guide you in reaching your annual goals. What is one step you can take next week that will be the foundation for you to reach one of your annual goals?

**Write It Down!**

> "Your written goals will guide you to not yield to new opportunities quickly. Opportunities can be viewed as distractions if they do not help you achieve your goals." ~Marki Lemons-Ryhal

There are many other benefits that you will enjoy when you write down your goals. First, it will give you a clear vision of what you want. From there, you will be able to take the necessary actions needed to achieve each goal. It's just like if you were to build your dream house: You don't just tell your architect and builder to build it exactly how you imagine it.

They need to have written plans and permits to get started. The same written plan is needed for developing and achieving your goals.

Goals let you see how well you are performing and allow you to celebrate your progress.

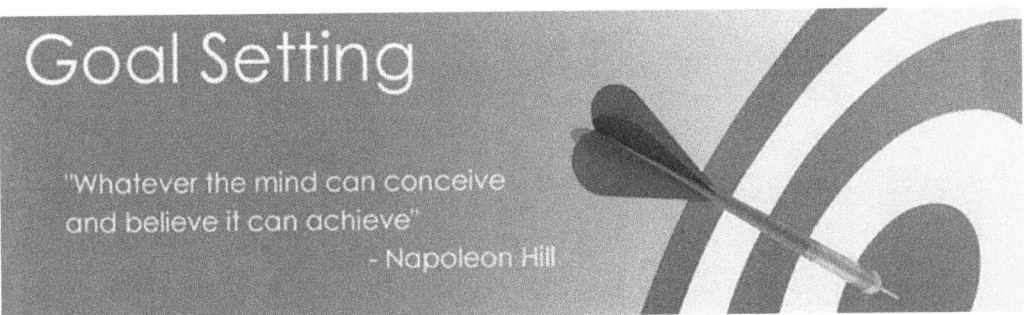

**Is Your Business Social Enough?**

Today, social media platforms have come to dominate our public consciousness. Social media has become a big part of our day-to-day routines and is an essential communication tool for people to connect and stay in touch. Consumers have turned to social media as one of the integral tools to determine a company's legitimacy, credibility, and viability. Businesses today are judged based on their online profiles. Consumers expect companies to respond to their concerns immediately.

Social media has managed to garnish market share and spending from traditional marketing methods. Modern marketing strategies use a mix of social media tactics and traditional methods as an integral component for reaching their business goals.

What S.M.A.R.T. goals do you want to accomplish over the next 66 days? Write down your goals and take action daily.

# SMART

   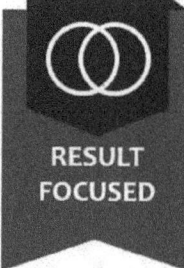 

SPECIFIC    MEASURABLE    ACHIEVABLE    RESULT FOCUSED    TIME BOUND

| | | |
|---|---|---|
| **S** | MAKE THEM SPECIFIC | |
| **M** | MAKE THEM MEASURABLE | |
| **A** | MAKE THEM ACHIEVABLE | |
| **R** | MAKE THEM RESULT FOCUSED | |
| **T** | MAKE THEM TIME BOUND | |

Date _____ /_____ /_____

**My Morning Routine**

1)_____
2)_____
3)_____
4)_____
5)_____


**How did you prospect for NEW business today?**

_____
_____
_____
_____
_____

How many calls, texts, emails, mobile business cards and handwritten notes did you send out today?

| Calls | Texts | Emails | Mobile Business Cards | Handwritten Notes |
|---|---|---|---|---|
|  |  |  |  |  |

What did you post today? Blog post, picture, video, or new idea?
_____
_____
_____

What value did you deliver today that sets you apart and makes you different from everyone else?
_____
_____
_____

What is one thing you learned today?
_____
_____
_____

What is one thing you struggled with today?
_____
_____
_____

COSNOP = Concentrate on Solutions Not on the Problem

What solutions can help you overcome your struggle?
_____
_____
_____

**Date** _____ / _____ / _____

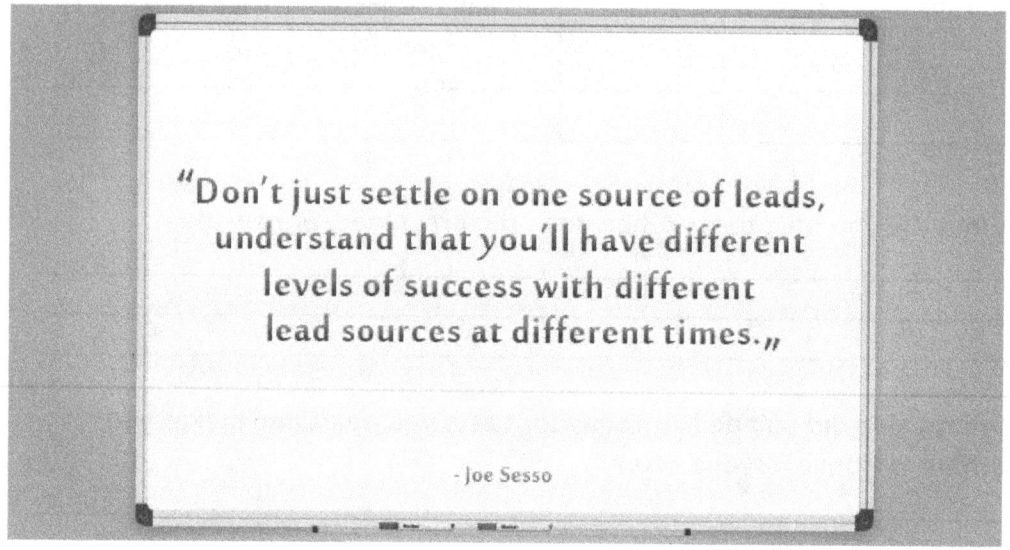

**My Morning Routine**

1)_____
2)_____
3)_____
4)_____
5)_____

**How did you prospect for NEW business today?**

_____
_____
_____
_____
_____

How many calls, texts, emails, mobile business cards and handwritten notes did you send out today?

| Calls | Texts | Emails | Mobile Business Cards | Handwritten Notes |
|-------|-------|--------|----------------------|-------------------|
|       |       |        |                      |                   |

What did you post today? Blog post, picture, video, or new idea?
_____
_____
_____

What value did you deliver today that sets you apart and makes you different from everyone else?
_____
_____
_____

What is one thing you learned today?
_____
_____
_____

What is one thing you struggled with today?
_____
_____
_____

### COSNOP = Concentrate on Solutions Not on the Problem

What solutions can help you overcome your struggle?
_____
_____
_____

Date \_\_\_\_ / \_\_\_\_ / \_\_\_\_

> *IT'S REALLY ABOUT FIGURING OUT WHAT YOU ARE, WHAT YOUR BRAND REPRESENTS, AND THEN CREATING CONTENT AROUND THAT BRAND TARGETING THE CORRECT AUDIENCE.*
> *— JUSTIN BARR.*

**My Morning Routine**

1)_____
2)_____
3)_____
4)_____
5)_____

**How did you prospect for NEW business today?**

_____
_____
_____
_____
_____

How many calls, texts, emails, mobile business cards and handwritten notes did you send out today?

| Calls | Texts | Emails | Mobile Business Cards | Handwritten Notes |
|-------|-------|--------|----------------------|-------------------|
|       |       |        |                      |                   |

What did you post today? Blog post, picture, video, or new idea?
_____
_____
_____

What value did you deliver today that sets you apart and makes you different from everyone else?
_____
_____
_____

What is one thing you learned today?
_____
_____
_____

What is one thing you struggled with today?
_____
_____
_____

COSNOP = Concentrate on Solutions Not on the Problem

What solutions can help you overcome your struggle?
_____
_____
_____

Date _____ / _____ / _____

> "Be consistent with it, it takes time and it's not something that happens overnight but if you're consistent it will pay you back."
>
> - Katelyn Montrony

**My Morning Routine**

1) _____
2) _____
3) _____
4) _____
5) _____

**How did you prospect for NEW business today?**

_____
_____
_____
_____
_____

How many calls, texts, emails, mobile business cards and handwritten notes did you send out today?

| Calls | Texts | Emails | Mobile Business Cards | Handwritten Notes |
|---|---|---|---|---|
|  |  |  |  |  |

What did you post today? Blog post, picture, video, or new idea?
_____
_____
_____

What value did you deliver today that sets you apart and makes you different from everyone else?
_____
_____
_____

What is one thing you learned today?
_____
_____
_____

What is one thing you struggled with today?
_____
_____
_____

### COSNOP = Concentrate on Solutions Not on the Problem

What solutions can help you overcome your struggle?
_____
_____
_____

Date _____ / _____ / _____

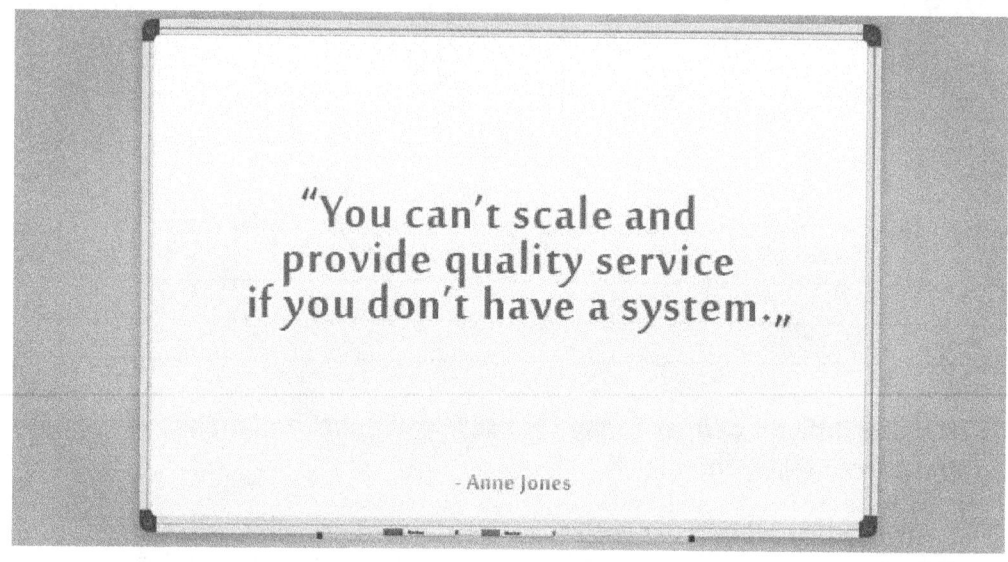

**My Morning Routine**

1)_____
2)_____
3)_____
4)_____
5)_____


**How did you prospect for NEW business today?**

_____
_____
_____
_____
_____

How many calls, texts, emails, mobile business cards and handwritten notes did you send out today?

| Calls | Texts | Emails | Mobile Business Cards | Handwritten Notes |
|---|---|---|---|---|
|  |  |  |  |  |

What did you post today? Blog post, picture, video, or new idea?
_____
_____
_____

What value did you deliver today that sets you apart and makes you different from everyone else?
_____
_____
_____

What is one thing you learned today?
_____
_____
_____

What is one thing you struggled with today?
_____
_____
_____

COSNOP = Concentrate on Solutions Not on the Problem

What solutions can help you overcome your struggle?
_____
_____
_____

Date _____ / _____ / _____

*"You can't be lazy, preparation is essential to success."*
— Marki Lemons-Ryhal

**My Morning Routine**

1) _____
2) _____
3) _____
4) _____
5) _____

**How did you prospect for NEW business today?**

_____
_____
_____
_____
_____

How many calls, texts, emails, mobile business cards and handwritten notes did you send out today?

| Calls | Texts | Emails | Mobile Business Cards | Handwritten Notes |
|-------|-------|--------|----------------------|-------------------|
|       |       |        |                      |                   |

What did you post today? Blog post, picture, video, or new idea?
_____
_____
_____

What value did you deliver today that sets you apart and makes you different from everyone else?
_____
_____
_____

What is one thing you learned today?
_____
_____
_____

What is one thing you struggled with today?
_____
_____
_____

### COSNOP = Concentrate on Solutions Not on the Problem

What solutions can help you overcome your struggle?
_____
_____
_____

Date _____ / _____ / _____

> "Marketing is all about awareness and attention. Facebook and Instagram give us attention, access and accuracy."
>
> - Tristen Sutton

**My Morning Routine**

1) _____
2) _____
3) _____
4) _____
5) _____


**How did you prospect for NEW business today?**

_____
_____
_____
_____
_____

How many calls, texts, emails, mobile business cards and handwritten notes did you send out today?

| Calls | Texts | Emails | Mobile Business Cards | Handwritten Notes |
|---|---|---|---|---|
|  |  |  |  |  |

What did you post today? Blog post, picture, video, or new idea?
_____
_____
_____

What value did you deliver today that sets you apart and makes you different from everyone else?
_____
_____
_____

What is one thing you learned today?
_____
_____
_____

What is one thing you struggled with today?
_____
_____
_____

**COSNOP = Concentrate on Solutions Not on the Problem**

What solutions can help you overcome your struggle?
_____
_____
_____

Date _____ / _____ / _____

# THE GOAL
## of a chatbot isn't to replicate or
### REPLACE THE CONVERSATION—IT'S TO START THE CONVERSATION.
*—zach hammer*

**My Morning Routine**

1) _____
2) _____
3) _____
4) _____
5) _____

**How did you prospect for NEW business today?**

_____
_____
_____
_____
_____

How many calls, texts, emails, mobile business cards and handwritten notes did you send out today?

| Calls | Texts | Emails | Mobile Business Cards | Handwritten Notes |
|-------|-------|--------|----------------------|-------------------|
|       |       |        |                      |                   |

What did you post today? Blog post, picture, video, or new idea?
_____
_____
_____

What value did you deliver today that sets you apart and makes you different from everyone else?
_____
_____
_____

What is one thing you learned today?
_____
_____
_____

What is one thing you struggled with today?
_____
_____
_____

### COSNOP = Concentrate on Solutions Not on the Problem

What solutions can help you overcome your struggle?
_____
_____
_____

**Date** _____ / _____ / _____

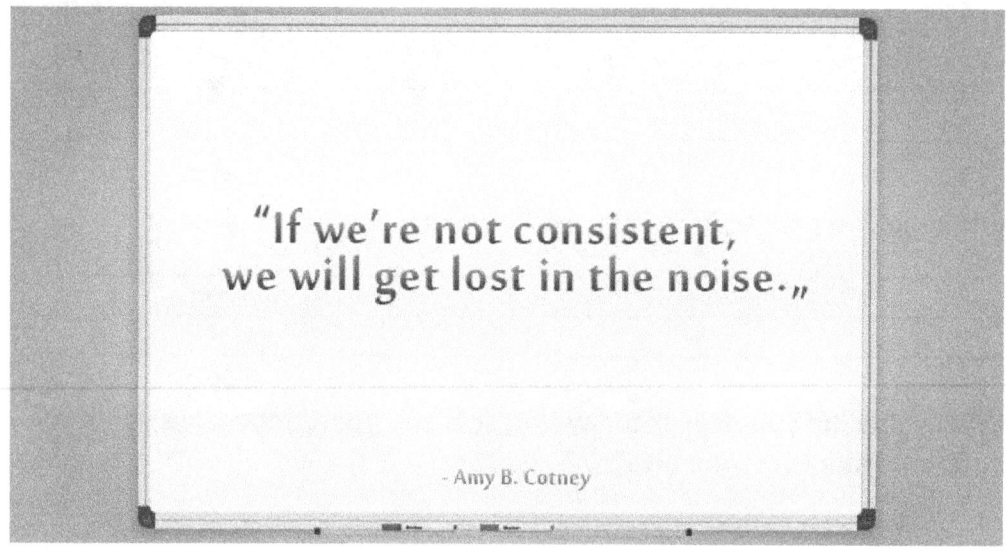

**My Morning Routine**

1)_____
2)_____
3)_____
4)_____
5)_____

**How did you prospect for NEW business today?**

_____
_____
_____
_____
_____

How many calls, texts, emails, mobile business cards and handwritten notes did you send out today?

| Calls | Texts | Emails | Mobile Business Cards | Handwritten Notes |
|-------|-------|--------|----------------------|-------------------|
|       |       |        |                      |                   |

What did you post today? Blog post, picture, video, or new idea?
_____
_____
_____

What value did you deliver today that sets you apart and makes you different from everyone else?
_____
_____
_____

What is one thing you learned today?
_____
_____
_____

What is one thing you struggled with today?
_____
_____
_____

COSNOP = Concentrate on Solutions Not on the Problem

What solutions can help you overcome your struggle?
_____
_____
_____

Date _____ / _____ / _____

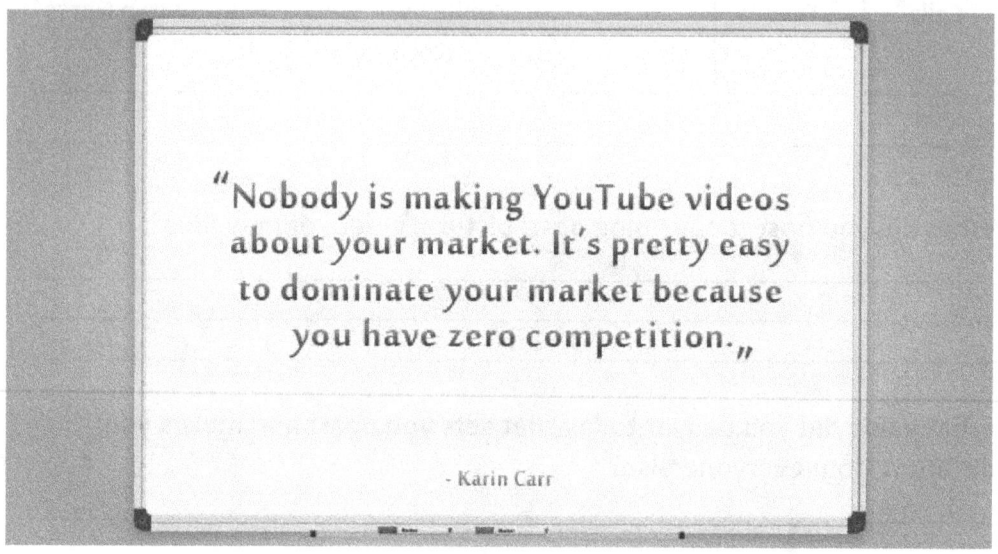

## My Morning Routine

1)_____
2)_____
3)_____
4)_____
5)_____


## How did you prospect for NEW business today?

_____
_____
_____
_____
_____

How many calls, texts, emails, mobile business cards and handwritten notes did you send out today?

| Calls | Texts | Emails | Mobile Business Cards | Handwritten Notes |
|-------|-------|--------|----------------------|-------------------|
|       |       |        |                      |                   |

What did you post today? Blog post, picture, video, or new idea?
_____
_____
_____

What value did you deliver today that sets you apart and makes you different from everyone else?
_____
_____
_____

What is one thing you learned today?
_____
_____
_____

What is one thing you struggled with today?
_____
_____
_____

### COSNOP = Concentrate on Solutions Not on the Problem

What solutions can help you overcome your struggle?
_____
_____
_____

Date _____ /_____ /_____

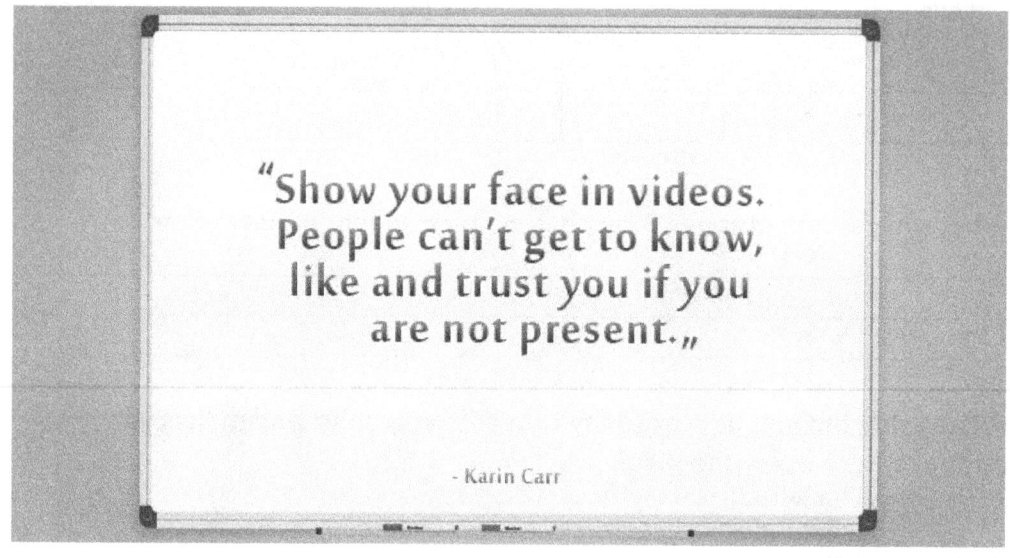

**My Morning Routine**

1)_____
2)_____
3)_____
4)_____
5)_____


**How did you prospect for NEW business today?**

_____
_____
_____
_____
_____

How many calls, texts, emails, mobile business cards and handwritten notes did you send out today?

| Calls | Texts | Emails | Mobile Business Cards | Handwritten Notes |
|-------|-------|--------|----------------------|-------------------|
|       |       |        |                      |                   |

What did you post today? Blog post, picture, video, or new idea?
_____
_____
_____

What value did you deliver today that sets you apart and makes you different from everyone else?
_____
_____
_____

What is one thing you learned today?
_____
_____
_____

What is one thing you struggled with today?
_____
_____
_____

**COSNOP = Concentrate on Solutions Not on the Problem**

What solutions can help you overcome your struggle?
_____
_____
_____

Date _____ /_____ /_____

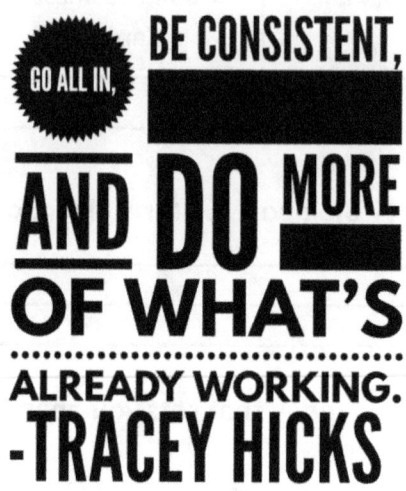

**My Morning Routine**

1)_____
2)_____
3)_____
4)_____
5)_____


**How did you prospect for NEW business today?**

_____
_____
_____
_____
_____

How many calls, texts, emails, mobile business cards and handwritten notes did you send out today?

| Calls | Texts | Emails | Mobile Business Cards | Handwritten Notes |
|-------|-------|--------|----------------------|-------------------|
|       |       |        |                      |                   |

What did you post today? Blog post, picture, video, or new idea?
_____
_____
_____

What value did you deliver today that sets you apart and makes you different from everyone else?
_____
_____
_____

What is one thing you learned today?
_____
_____
_____

What is one thing you struggled with today?
_____
_____
_____

**COSNOP = Concentrate on Solutions Not on the Problem**

What solutions can help you overcome your struggle?
_____
_____
_____

**Date** _____ / _____ / _____

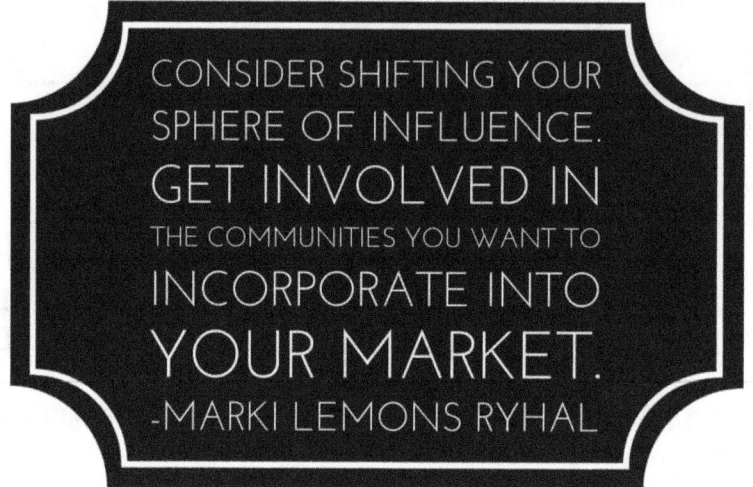

CONSIDER SHIFTING YOUR SPHERE OF INFLUENCE. GET INVOLVED IN THE COMMUNITIES YOU WANT TO INCORPORATE INTO YOUR MARKET.
-MARKI LEMONS RYHAL

**My Morning Routine**

1)_____
2)_____
3)_____
4)_____
5)_____

**How did you prospect for NEW business today?**

_____
_____
_____
_____
_____

How many calls, texts, emails, mobile business cards and handwritten notes did you send out today?

| Calls | Texts | Emails | Mobile Business Cards | Handwritten Notes |
|-------|-------|--------|----------------------|-------------------|
|       |       |        |                      |                   |

What did you post today? Blog post, picture, video, or new idea?
_____
_____
_____

What value did you deliver today that sets you apart and makes you different from everyone else?
_____
_____
_____

What is one thing you learned today?
_____
_____
_____

What is one thing you struggled with today?
_____
_____
_____

**COSNOP = Concentrate on Solutions Not on the Problem**

What solutions can help you overcome your struggle?
_____
_____
_____

Date _____ / _____ / _____

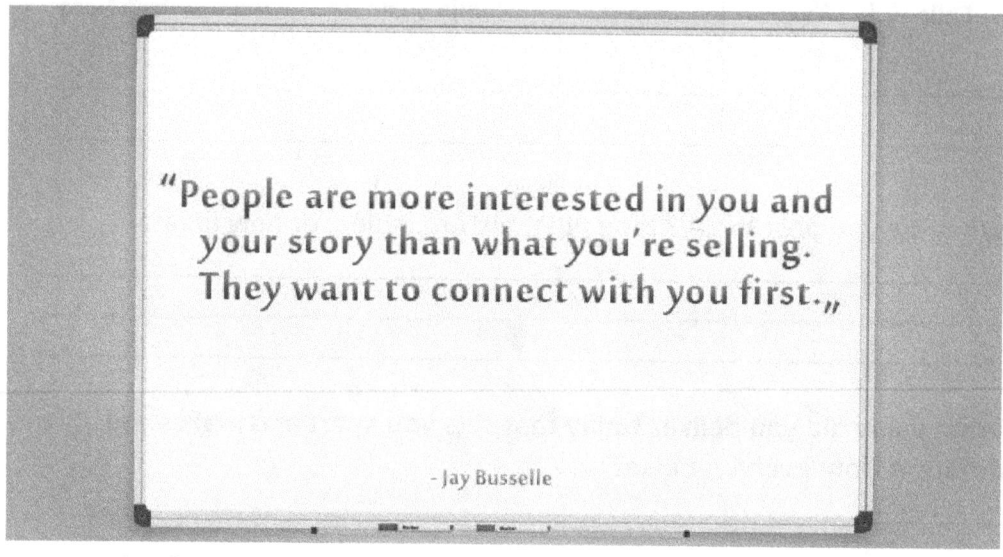

"People are more interested in you and your story than what you're selling. They want to connect with you first."

- Jay Busselle

**My Morning Routine**

1)_____
2)_____
3)_____
4)_____
5)_____


**How did you prospect for NEW business today?**

_____
_____
_____
_____
_____

How many calls, texts, emails, mobile business cards and handwritten notes did you send out today?

| Calls | Texts | Emails | Mobile Business Cards | Handwritten Notes |
|---|---|---|---|---|
|  |  |  |  |  |

What did you post today? Blog post, picture, video, or new idea?
_____
_____
_____

What value did you deliver today that sets you apart and makes you different from everyone else?
_____
_____
_____

What is one thing you learned today?
_____
_____
_____

What is one thing you struggled with today?
_____
_____
_____

### COSNOP = Concentrate on Solutions Not on the Problem

What solutions can help you overcome your struggle?
_____
_____
_____

Date _____ /_____ /_____

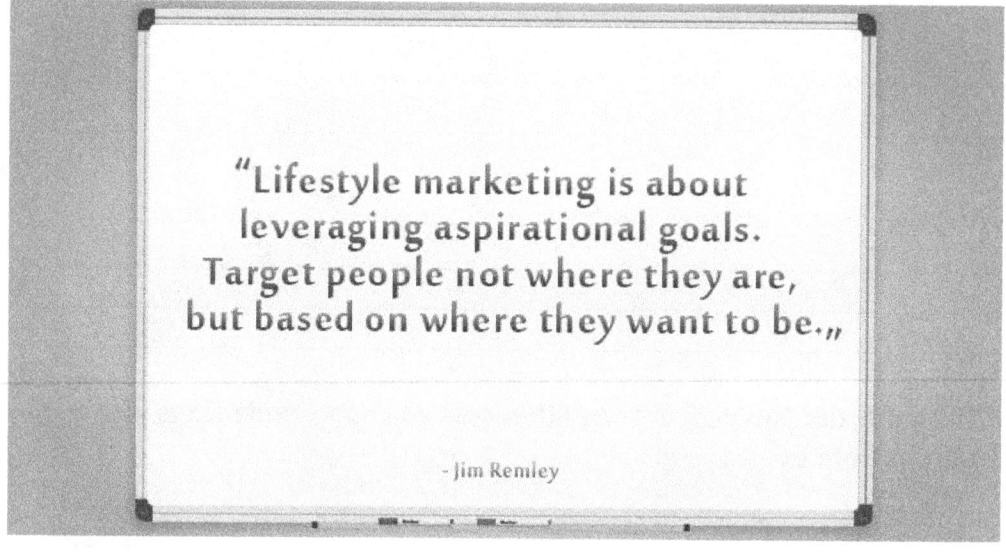

**My Morning Routine**

1)_____
2)_____
3)_____
4)_____
5)_____


**How did you prospect for NEW business today?**

_____
_____
_____
_____
_____

How many calls, texts, emails, mobile business cards and handwritten notes did you send out today?

| Calls | Texts | Emails | Mobile Business Cards | Handwritten Notes |
|---|---|---|---|---|
|  |  |  |  |  |

What did you post today? Blog post, picture, video, or new idea?
_____
_____
_____

What value did you deliver today that sets you apart and makes you different from everyone else?
_____
_____
_____

What is one thing you learned today?
_____
_____
_____

What is one thing you struggled with today?
_____
_____
_____

COSNOP = Concentrate on Solutions Not on the Problem

What solutions can help you overcome your struggle?
_____
_____
_____

**Date** _____ / _____ / _____

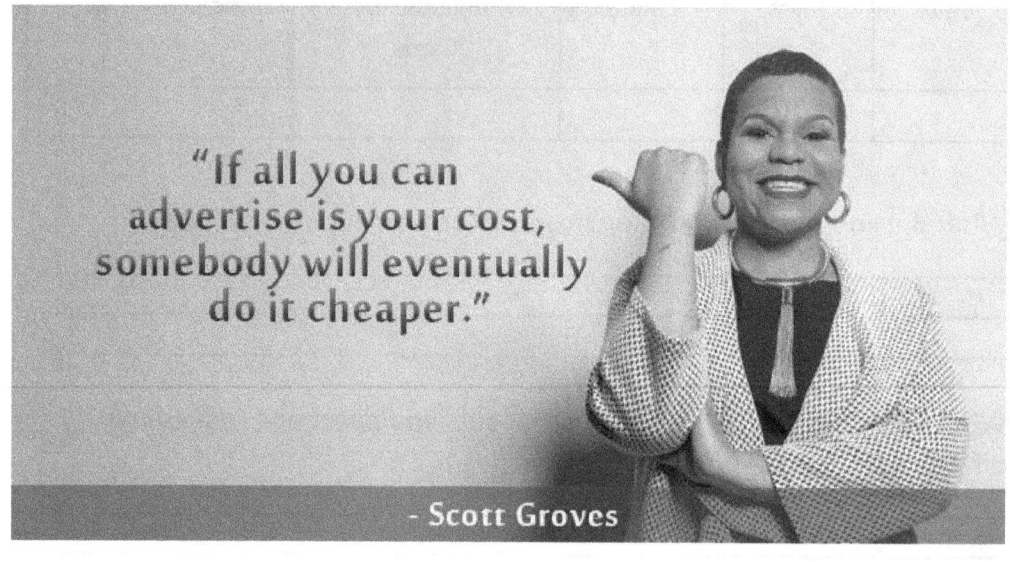

**My Morning Routine**

1)_____

2)_____

3)_____

4)_____

5)_____


**How did you prospect for NEW business today?**

_____
_____
_____
_____
_____

How many calls, texts, emails, mobile business cards and handwritten notes did you send out today?

| Calls | Texts | Emails | Mobile Business Cards | Handwritten Notes |
|-------|-------|--------|----------------------|-------------------|
|       |       |        |                      |                   |

What did you post today? Blog post, picture, video, or new idea?
_____
_____
_____

What value did you deliver today that sets you apart and makes you different from everyone else?
_____
_____
_____

What is one thing you learned today?
_____
_____
_____

What is one thing you struggled with today?
_____
_____
_____

COSNOP = Concentrate on Solutions Not on the Problem

What solutions can help you overcome your struggle?
_____
_____
_____

Date _____ /_____ /_____

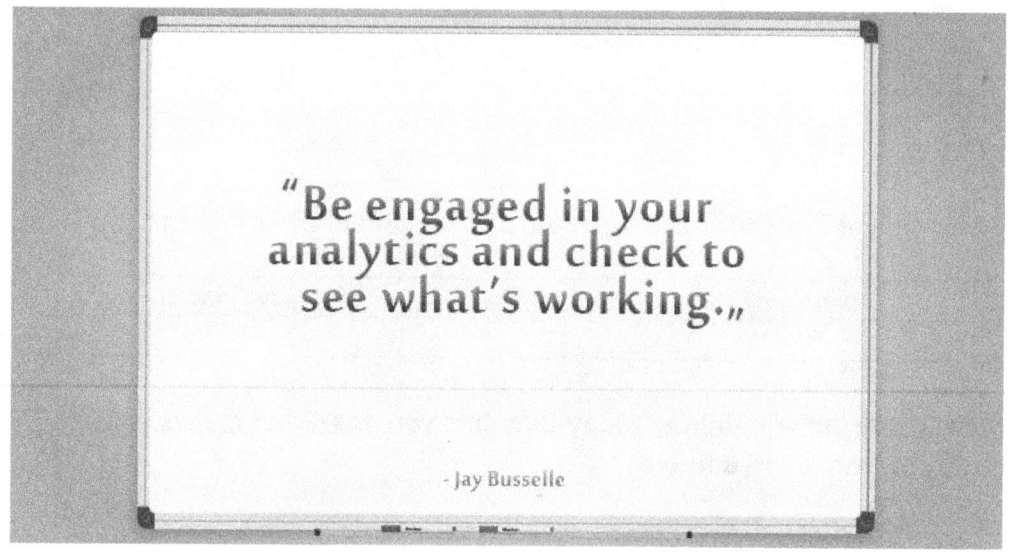

**My Morning Routine**

1)_____
2)_____
3)_____
4)_____
5)_____

**How did you prospect for NEW business today?**

_____
_____
_____
_____
_____

How many calls, texts, emails, mobile business cards and handwritten notes did you send out today?

| Calls | Texts | Emails | Mobile Business Cards | Handwritten Notes |
|-------|-------|--------|----------------------|-------------------|
|       |       |        |                      |                   |

What did you post today? Blog post, picture, video, or new idea?
_____
_____
_____

What value did you deliver today that sets you apart and makes you different from everyone else?
_____
_____
_____

What is one thing you learned today?
_____
_____
_____

What is one thing you struggled with today?
_____
_____
_____

COSNOP = Concentrate on Solutions Not on the Problem

What solutions can help you overcome your struggle?
_____
_____
_____

Date _____ / _____ / _____

> *Create video content.*
> **VIDEOS ARE** THE MOST POPULAR CONTENT ON **THE INTERNET,** *and will continue to be in the foreseeable future.*
> *–Marki Lemons-Ryhal*

**My Morning Routine**

1) _____
2) _____
3) _____
4) _____
5) _____

**How did you prospect for NEW business today?**

_____
_____
_____
_____
_____

How many calls, texts, emails, mobile business cards and handwritten notes did you send out today?

| Calls | Texts | Emails | Mobile Business Cards | Handwritten Notes |
|-------|-------|--------|----------------------|-------------------|
|       |       |        |                      |                   |

What did you post today? Blog post, picture, video, or new idea?
_____
_____
_____

What value did you deliver today that sets you apart and makes you different from everyone else?
_____
_____
_____

What is one thing you learned today?
_____
_____
_____

What is one thing you struggled with today?
_____
_____
_____

**COSNOP = Concentrate on Solutions Not on the Problem**

What solutions can help you overcome your struggle?
_____
_____
_____

Date _____ / _____ / _____

> "If you're targeting the content you're delivering to people correctly, send them down the right follow up funnel."
>
> -Alex Camelio

**My Morning Routine**

1) _____
2) _____
3) _____
4) _____
5) _____

**How did you prospect for NEW business today?**

_____
_____
_____
_____
_____

How many calls, texts, emails, mobile business cards and handwritten notes did you send out today?

| Calls | Texts | Emails | Mobile Business Cards | Handwritten Notes |
|-------|-------|--------|----------------------|-------------------|
|       |       |        |                      |                   |

What did you post today? Blog post, picture, video, or new idea?
_____
_____
_____

What value did you deliver today that sets you apart and makes you different from everyone else?
_____
_____
_____

What is one thing you learned today?
_____
_____
_____

What is one thing you struggled with today?
_____
_____
_____

## COSNOP = Concentrate on Solutions Not on the Problem

What solutions can help you overcome your struggle?
_____
_____
_____

Date _____ /_____ /_____

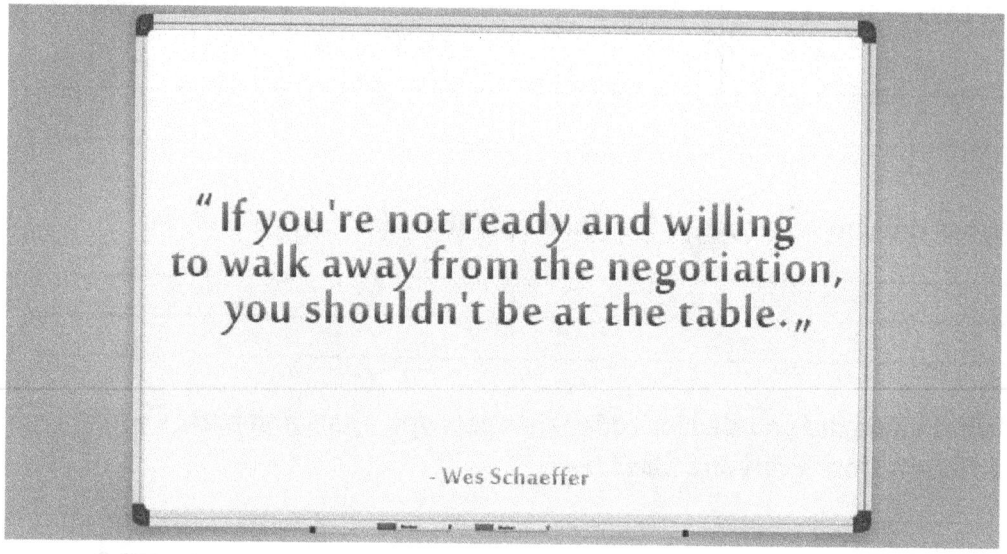

**My Morning Routine**

1)_____
2)_____
3)_____
4)_____
5)_____


**How did you prospect for NEW business today?**

_____
_____
_____
_____
_____

How many calls, texts, emails, mobile business cards and handwritten notes did you send out today?

| Calls | Texts | Emails | Mobile Business Cards | Handwritten Notes |
|-------|-------|--------|----------------------|-------------------|
|       |       |        |                      |                   |

What did you post today? Blog post, picture, video, or new idea?
_____
_____
_____

What value did you deliver today that sets you apart and makes you different from everyone else?
_____
_____
_____

What is one thing you learned today?
_____
_____
_____

What is one thing you struggled with today?
_____
_____
_____

COSNOP = Concentrate on Solutions Not on the Problem

What solutions can help you overcome your struggle?
_____
_____
_____

Date _____ /_____ /_____

— Steve Werner

**My Morning Routine**

1)_____
2)_____
3)_____
4)_____
5)_____


**How did you prospect for NEW business today?**

_____
_____
_____
_____
_____

How many calls, texts, emails, mobile business cards and handwritten notes did you send out today?

| Calls | Texts | Emails | Mobile Business Cards | Handwritten Notes |
|-------|-------|--------|-----------------------|-------------------|
|       |       |        |                       |                   |

What did you post today? Blog post, picture, video, or new idea?
_____
_____
_____

What value did you deliver today that sets you apart and makes you different from everyone else?
_____
_____
_____

What is one thing you learned today?
_____
_____
_____

What is one thing you struggled with today?
_____
_____
_____

COSNOP = Concentrate on Solutions Not on the Problem

What solutions can help you overcome your struggle?
_____
_____
_____

Date _____ / _____ / _____

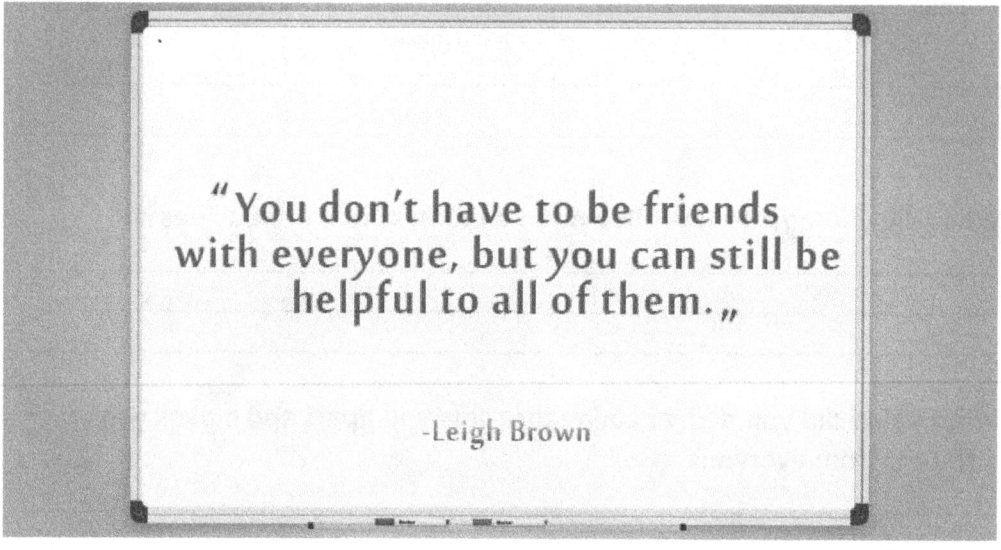

**My Morning Routine**

1)_____
2)_____
3)_____
4)_____
5)_____


**How did you prospect for NEW business today?**

_____
_____
_____
_____
_____

How many calls, texts, emails, mobile business cards and handwritten notes did you send out today?

| Calls | Texts | Emails | Mobile Business Cards | Handwritten Notes |
|-------|-------|--------|----------------------|-------------------|
|       |       |        |                      |                   |

What did you post today? Blog post, picture, video, or new idea?
_____
_____
_____

What value did you deliver today that sets you apart and makes you different from everyone else?
_____
_____
_____

What is one thing you learned today?
_____
_____
_____

What is one thing you struggled with today?
_____
_____
_____

### COSNOP = Concentrate on Solutions Not on the Problem

What solutions can help you overcome your struggle?
_____
_____
_____

Date _____ / _____ / _____

> **STOP WORRYING ABOUT HOW YOU LOOK IN YOUR VIDEOS. INSTEAD, ENSURE YOUR CONTENT SERVES THE NEEDS OF YOUR AUDIENCE.**
> —MARKI LEMONS-RYHAL

**My Morning Routine**

1) _____
2) _____
3) _____
4) _____
5) _____

**How did you prospect for NEW business today?**

_____
_____
_____
_____
_____

How many calls, texts, emails, mobile business cards and handwritten notes did you send out today?

| Calls | Texts | Emails | Mobile Business Cards | Handwritten Notes |
|---|---|---|---|---|
|  |  |  |  |  |

What did you post today? Blog post, picture, video, or new idea?
_____
_____
_____

What value did you deliver today that sets you apart and makes you different from everyone else?
_____
_____
_____

What is one thing you learned today?
_____
_____
_____

What is one thing you struggled with today?
_____
_____
_____

COSNOP = Concentrate on Solutions Not on the Problem

What solutions can help you overcome your struggle?
_____
_____
_____

Date _____ / _____ / _____

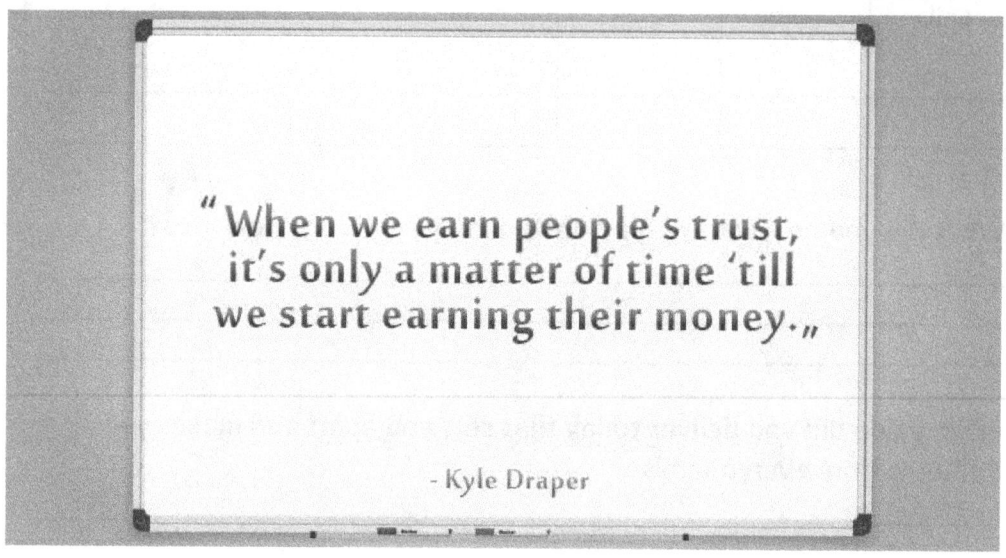

My Morning Routine

1)_____
2)_____
3)_____
4)_____
5)_____


How did you prospect for NEW business today?

_____
_____
_____
_____
_____

How many calls, texts, emails, mobile business cards and handwritten notes did you send out today?

| Calls | Texts | Emails | Mobile Business Cards | Handwritten Notes |
|---|---|---|---|---|
|  |  |  |  |  |

What did you post today? Blog post, picture, video, or new idea?
_____
_____
_____

What value did you deliver today that sets you apart and makes you different from everyone else?
_____
_____
_____

What is one thing you learned today?
_____
_____
_____

What is one thing you struggled with today?
_____
_____
_____

**COSNOP = Concentrate on Solutions Not on the Problem**

What solutions can help you overcome your struggle?
_____
_____
_____

Date _____ /_____ /_____

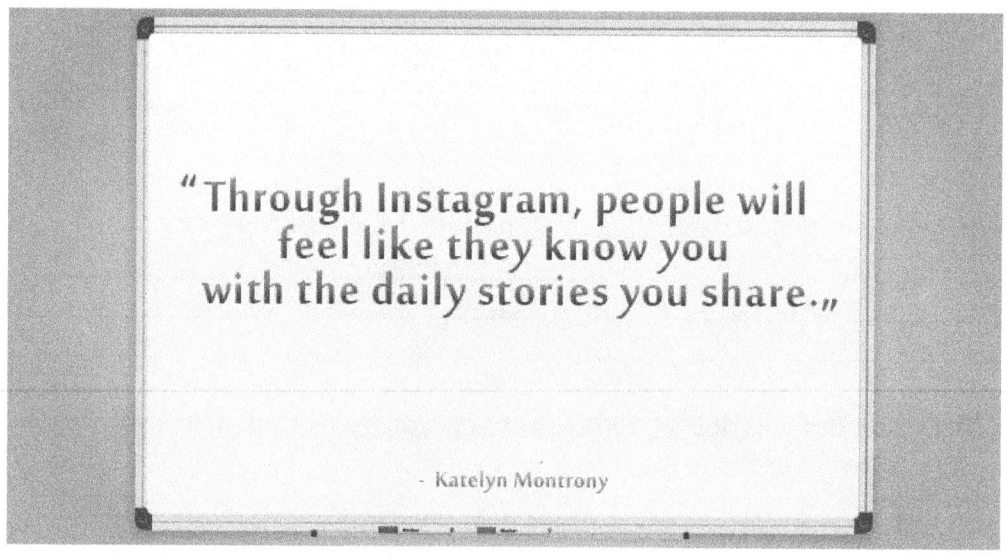

**My Morning Routine**

1)_____
2)_____
3)_____
4)_____
5)_____


**How did you prospect for NEW business today?**

_____
_____
_____
_____
_____

How many calls, texts, emails, mobile business cards and handwritten notes did you send out today?

| Calls | Texts | Emails | Mobile Business Cards | Handwritten Notes |
|-------|-------|--------|----------------------|-------------------|
|       |       |        |                      |                   |

What did you post today? Blog post, picture, video, or new idea?
_____
_____
_____

What value did you deliver today that sets you apart and makes you different from everyone else?
_____
_____
_____

What is one thing you learned today?
_____
_____
_____

What is one thing you struggled with today?
_____
_____
_____

**COSNOP = Concentrate on Solutions Not on the Problem**

What solutions can help you overcome your struggle?
_____
_____
_____

**Date** _____ / _____ / _____

"You can't just post content and expect people to reach out to you. They're waiting for us to reach out to them, and they'll have a conversation with us if we kick it off."

Matt Johnson

**My Morning Routine**

1)_____
2)_____
3)_____
4)_____
5)_____


**How did you prospect for NEW business today?**

_____
_____
_____
_____
_____

How many calls, texts, emails, mobile business cards and handwritten notes did you send out today?

| Calls | Texts | Emails | Mobile Business Cards | Handwritten Notes |
|-------|-------|--------|-----------------------|-------------------|
|       |       |        |                       |                   |

What did you post today? Blog post, picture, video, or new idea?
_____
_____
_____

What value did you deliver today that sets you apart and makes you different from everyone else?
_____
_____
_____

What is one thing you learned today?
_____
_____
_____

What is one thing you struggled with today?
_____
_____
_____

**COSNOP = Concentrate on Solutions Not on the Problem**

What solutions can help you overcome your struggle?
_____
_____
_____

Date _____ /_____ /_____

> "LinkedIn is now trying to position itself as a media company, and a content creation platform. They are doing all they can to get more people on the platform."
>
> - Deborrah Ashley

**My Morning Routine**

1)_____
2)_____
3)_____
4)_____
5)_____


**How did you prospect for NEW business today?**

_____
_____
_____
_____
_____

How many calls, texts, emails, mobile business cards and handwritten notes did you send out today?

| Calls | Texts | Emails | Mobile Business Cards | Handwritten Notes |
|---|---|---|---|---|
|  |  |  |  |  |

What did you post today? Blog post, picture, video, or new idea?
_____
_____
_____

What value did you deliver today that sets you apart and makes you different from everyone else?
_____
_____
_____

What is one thing you learned today?
_____
_____
_____

What is one thing you struggled with today?
_____
_____
_____

COSNOP = Concentrate on Solutions Not on the Problem

What solutions can help you overcome your struggle?
_____
_____
_____

Date _____ / _____ / _____

## SEEK PR OPPORTUNITIES IN YOUR LOCAL MARKET.

## YOU HAVE THE ABILITY TO STAND OUT AS A VALUABLE ASSET

## TO PUBLICATIONS IN THAT AREA.
### -CHRISTINA DAVES

**My Morning Routine**

1)_____

2)_____

3)_____

4)_____

5)_____


**How did you prospect for NEW business today?**

_____
_____
_____
_____
_____

How many calls, texts, emails, mobile business cards and handwritten notes did you send out today?

| Calls | Texts | Emails | Mobile Business Cards | Handwritten Notes |
|-------|-------|--------|----------------------|-------------------|
|       |       |        |                      |                   |

What did you post today? Blog post, picture, video, or new idea?
_____
_____
_____

What value did you deliver today that sets you apart and makes you different from everyone else?
_____
_____
_____

What is one thing you learned today?
_____
_____
_____

What is one thing you struggled with today?
_____
_____
_____

COSNOP = Concentrate on Solutions Not on the Problem

What solutions can help you overcome your struggle?
_____
_____
_____

**Date** _____ / _____ / _____

> "If you make a great video but you don't have a distribution plan, you haven't done anything."
>
> - Anne Jones

**My Morning Routine**

1) _____
2) _____
3) _____
4) _____
5) _____

**How did you prospect for NEW business today?**

_____
_____
_____
_____
_____

How many calls, texts, emails, mobile business cards and handwritten notes did you send out today?

| Calls | Texts | Emails | Mobile Business Cards | Handwritten Notes |
|-------|-------|--------|----------------------|-------------------|
|       |       |        |                      |                   |

What did you post today? Blog post, picture, video, or new idea?
_____
_____
_____

What value did you deliver today that sets you apart and makes you different from everyone else?
_____
_____
_____

What is one thing you learned today?
_____
_____
_____

What is one thing you struggled with today?
_____
_____
_____

COSNOP = Concentrate on Solutions Not on the Problem

What solutions can help you overcome your struggle?
_____
_____
_____

Date _____ /_____ /_____

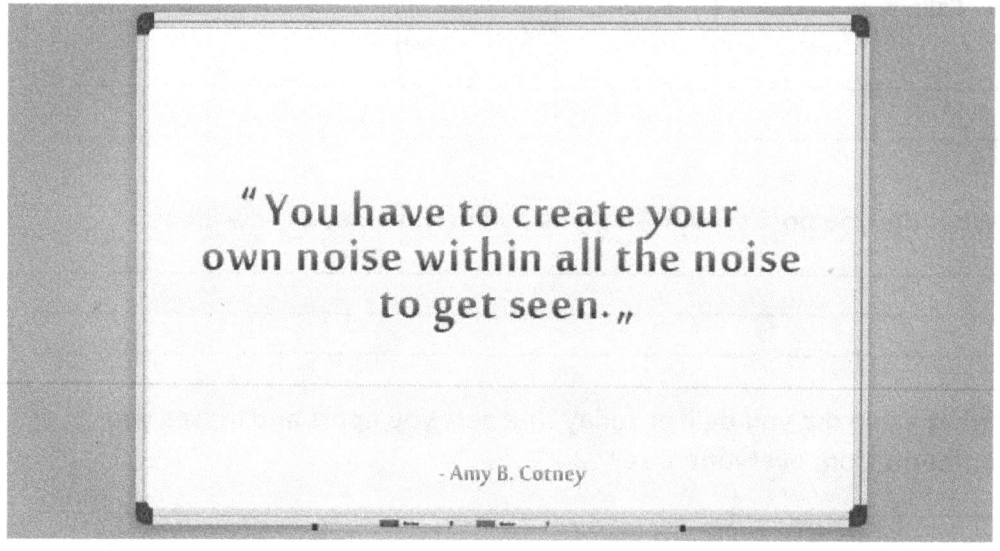

My Morning Routine

1)_____
2)_____
3)_____
4)_____
5)_____


How did you prospect for NEW business today?

_____
_____
_____
_____
_____

How many calls, texts, emails, mobile business cards and handwritten notes did you send out today?

| Calls | Texts | Emails | Mobile Business Cards | Handwritten Notes |
|---|---|---|---|---|
|  |  |  |  |  |

What did you post today? Blog post, picture, video, or new idea?
_____
_____
_____

What value did you deliver today that sets you apart and makes you different from everyone else?
_____
_____
_____

What is one thing you learned today?
_____
_____
_____

What is one thing you struggled with today?
_____
_____
_____

**COSNOP = Concentrate on Solutions Not on the Problem**

What solutions can help you overcome your struggle?
_____
_____
_____

Date _____ / _____ / _____

"They used to say a picture is worth a thousand words. Well, today one minute of video content is worth 1.8 million words. You should be creating those one-minute videos."

- Marki Lemons-Ryhal

**My Morning Routine**

1)_____
2)_____
3)_____
4)_____
5)_____


**How did you prospect for NEW business today?**

_____
_____
_____
_____
_____

How many calls, texts, emails, mobile business cards and handwritten notes did you send out today?

| Calls | Texts | Emails | Mobile Business Cards | Handwritten Notes |
|-------|-------|--------|-----------------------|-------------------|
|       |       |        |                       |                   |

What did you post today? Blog post, picture, video, or new idea?
_____
_____
_____

What value did you deliver today that sets you apart and makes you different from everyone else?
_____
_____
_____

What is one thing you learned today?
_____
_____
_____

What is one thing you struggled with today?
_____
_____
_____

### COSNOP = Concentrate on Solutions Not on the Problem

What solutions can help you overcome your struggle?
_____
_____
_____

**Date** _____ / _____ / _____

> "Resurrect the leads everyone else has written off. Keep them in your CRM and you'll be surprised at how many of them come alive."
>
> - Joe Sesso

**My Morning Routine**

1) _____
2) _____
3) _____
4) _____
5) _____

**How did you prospect for NEW business today?**

_____
_____
_____
_____
_____

How many calls, texts, emails, mobile business cards and handwritten notes did you send out today?

| Calls | Texts | Emails | Mobile Business Cards | Handwritten Notes |
|-------|-------|--------|----------------------|-------------------|
|       |       |        |                      |                   |

What did you post today? Blog post, picture, video, or new idea?
_____
_____
_____

What value did you deliver today that sets you apart and makes you different from everyone else?
_____
_____
_____

What is one thing you learned today?
_____
_____
_____

What is one thing you struggled with today?
_____
_____
_____

COSNOP = Concentrate on Solutions Not on the Problem

What solutions can help you overcome your struggle?
_____
_____
_____

Date _____ / _____ / _____

## YOU'VE GOT TO SHOW THAT YOU ARE AN EXPERT—IDEALLY IN A NICHE.
## -CHRISTINA DAVES

**My Morning Routine**

1) _____
2) _____
3) _____
4) _____
5) _____

**How did you prospect for NEW business today?**

_____
_____
_____
_____
_____

How many calls, texts, emails, mobile business cards and handwritten notes did you send out today?

| Calls | Texts | Emails | Mobile Business Cards | Handwritten Notes |
|---|---|---|---|---|
|  |  |  |  |  |

What did you post today? Blog post, picture, video, or new idea?
_____
_____
_____

What value did you deliver today that sets you apart and makes you different from everyone else?
_____
_____
_____

What is one thing you learned today?
_____
_____
_____

What is one thing you struggled with today?
_____
_____
_____

COSNOP = Concentrate on Solutions Not on the Problem

What solutions can help you overcome your struggle?
_____
_____
_____

Date _____ / _____ / _____

> "At the end of the day, nothing changes about the concept of connecting with people and delivering on what their needs are."
>
> - James Tyler

**My Morning Routine**

1) _____
2) _____
3) _____
4) _____
5) _____

**How did you prospect for NEW business today?**

_____
_____
_____
_____
_____

How many calls, texts, emails, mobile business cards and handwritten notes did you send out today?

| Calls | Texts | Emails | Mobile Business Cards | Handwritten Notes |
|-------|-------|--------|----------------------|-------------------|
|       |       |        |                      |                   |

What did you post today? Blog post, picture, video, or new idea?
_____
_____
_____

What value did you deliver today that sets you apart and makes you different from everyone else?
_____
_____
_____

What is one thing you learned today?
_____
_____
_____

What is one thing you struggled with today?
_____
_____
_____

**COSNOP = Concentrate on Solutions Not on the Problem**

What solutions can help you overcome your struggle?
_____
_____
_____

Date _____ / _____ / _____

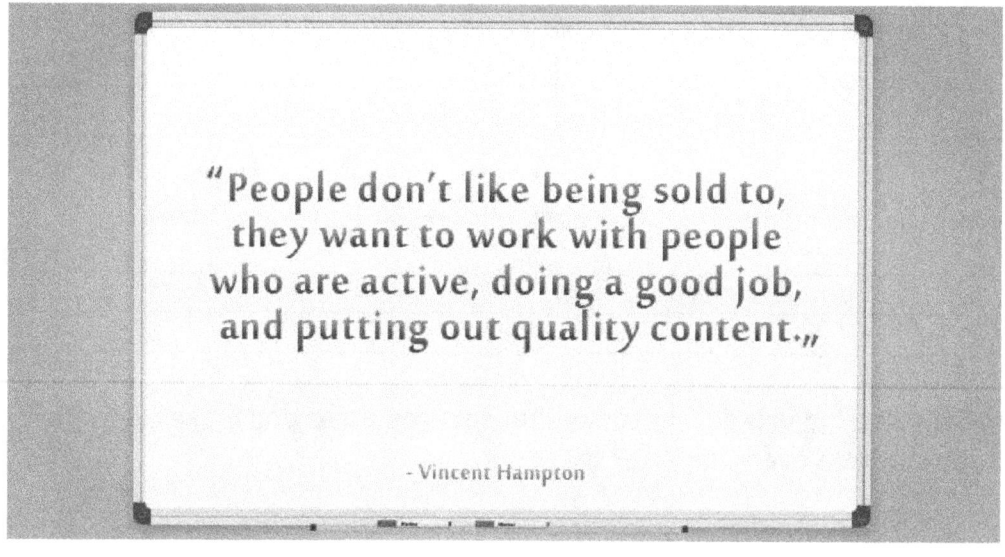

**My Morning Routine**

1)_____
2)_____
3)_____
4)_____
5)_____


**How did you prospect for NEW business today?**

_____
_____
_____
_____
_____

How many calls, texts, emails, mobile business cards and handwritten notes did you send out today?

| Calls | Texts | Emails | Mobile Business Cards | Handwritten Notes |
|-------|-------|--------|----------------------|-------------------|
|       |       |        |                      |                   |

What did you post today? Blog post, picture, video, or new idea?
_____
_____
_____

What value did you deliver today that sets you apart and makes you different from everyone else?
_____
_____
_____

What is one thing you learned today?
_____
_____
_____

What is one thing you struggled with today?
_____
_____
_____

COSNOP = Concentrate on Solutions Not on the Problem

What solutions can help you overcome your struggle?
_____
_____
_____

Date _____ /_____ /_____

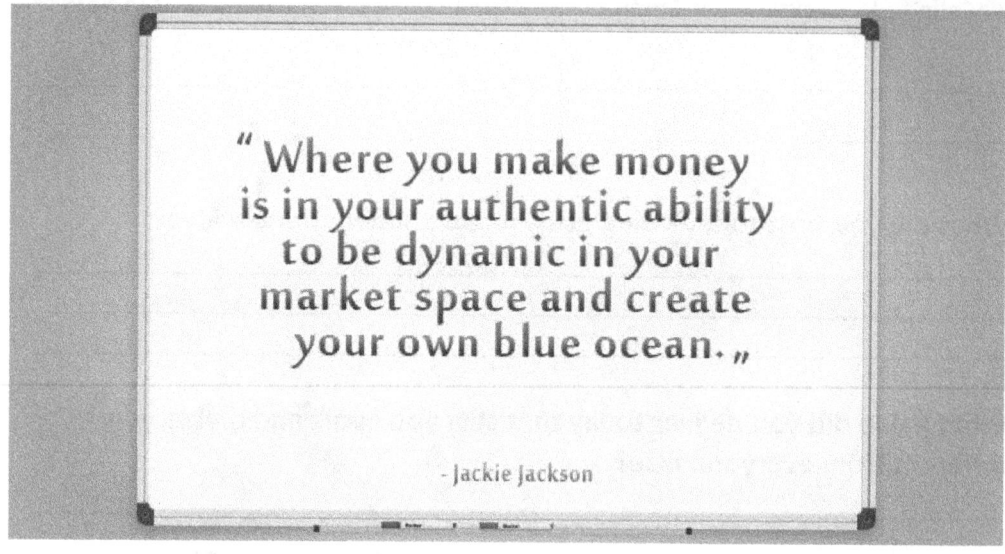

**My Morning Routine**

1)_____
2)_____
3)_____
4)_____
5)_____


**How did you prospect for NEW business today?**

_____
_____
_____
_____
_____

How many calls, texts, emails, mobile business cards and handwritten notes did you send out today?

| Calls | Texts | Emails | Mobile Business Cards | Handwritten Notes |
|-------|-------|--------|----------------------|-------------------|
|       |       |        |                      |                   |

What did you post today? Blog post, picture, video, or new idea?
_____
_____
_____

What value did you deliver today that sets you apart and makes you different from everyone else?
_____
_____
_____

What is one thing you learned today?
_____
_____
_____

What is one thing you struggled with today?
_____
_____
_____

**COSNOP = Concentrate on Solutions Not on the Problem**

What solutions can help you overcome your struggle?
_____
_____
_____

Date _____ / _____ / _____

> "Look at how you can use social media platforms to get in front of a specific market that has the highest demand for what you have to offer."
>
> - Karen Liz Albert

**My Morning Routine**

1) _____
2) _____
3) _____
4) _____
5) _____

**How did you prospect for NEW business today?**

_____
_____
_____
_____
_____

How many calls, texts, emails, mobile business cards and handwritten notes did you send out today?

| Calls | Texts | Emails | Mobile Business Cards | Handwritten Notes |
|-------|-------|--------|----------------------|-------------------|
|       |       |        |                      |                   |

What did you post today? Blog post, picture, video, or new idea?
_____
_____
_____

What value did you deliver today that sets you apart and makes you different from everyone else?
_____
_____
_____

What is one thing you learned today?
_____
_____
_____

What is one thing you struggled with today?
_____
_____
_____

COSNOP = Concentrate on Solutions Not on the Problem

What solutions can help you overcome your struggle?
_____
_____
_____

Date _____ / _____ / _____

**DON'T BE POOR: PASSING OVER OPPORTUNITIES REPEATEDLY.**

-CHAD DURFEE

**My Morning Routine**

1)_____
2)_____
3)_____
4)_____
5)_____

**How did you prospect for NEW business today?**

_____
_____
_____
_____
_____

How many calls, texts, emails, mobile business cards and handwritten notes did you send out today?

| Calls | Texts | Emails | Mobile Business Cards | Handwritten Notes |
|-------|-------|--------|----------------------|-------------------|
|       |       |        |                      |                   |

What did you post today? Blog post, picture, video, or new idea?
_____
_____
_____

What value did you deliver today that sets you apart and makes you different from everyone else?
_____
_____
_____

What is one thing you learned today?
_____
_____
_____

What is one thing you struggled with today?
_____
_____
_____

**COSNOP = Concentrate on Solutions Not on the Problem**

What solutions can help you overcome your struggle?
_____
_____
_____

Date _____ /_____ /_____

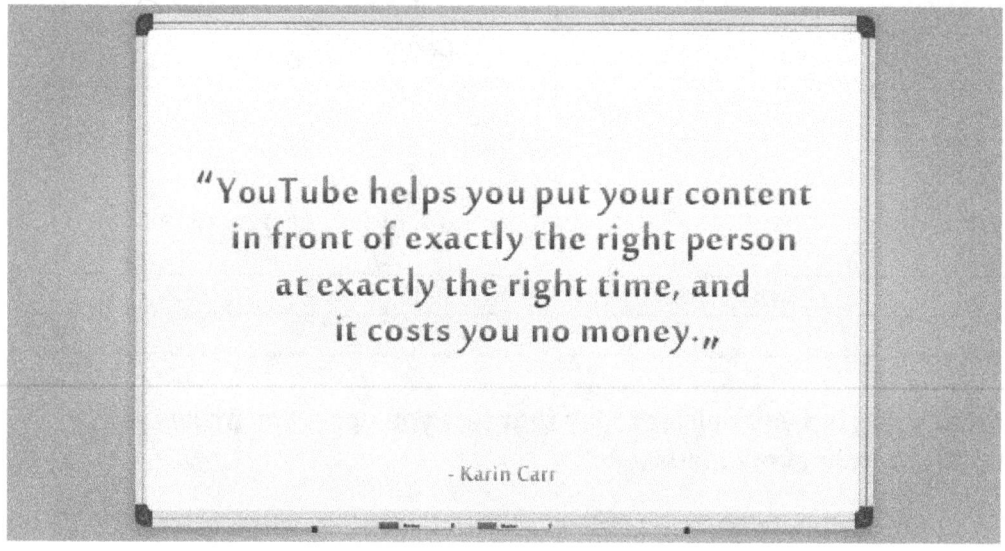

**My Morning Routine**

1)_____
2)_____
3)_____
4)_____
5)_____

**How did you prospect for NEW business today?**

_____
_____
_____
_____
_____

How many calls, texts, emails, mobile business cards and handwritten notes did you send out today?

| Calls | Texts | Emails | Mobile Business Cards | Handwritten Notes |
|-------|-------|--------|----------------------|-------------------|
|       |       |        |                      |                   |

What did you post today? Blog post, picture, video, or new idea?
_____
_____
_____

What value did you deliver today that sets you apart and makes you different from everyone else?
_____
_____
_____

What is one thing you learned today?
_____
_____
_____

What is one thing you struggled with today?
_____
_____
_____

**COSNOP = Concentrate on Solutions Not on the Problem**

What solutions can help you overcome your struggle?
_____
_____
_____

Date _____ / _____ / _____

> "The 3 key things required for success is work, discipline and commitment."
>
> - Anita AC Clinton

**My Morning Routine**

1) _____
2) _____
3) _____
4) _____
5) _____

**How did you prospect for NEW business today?**

_____
_____
_____
_____
_____

How many calls, texts, emails, mobile business cards and handwritten notes did you send out today?

| Calls | Texts | Emails | Mobile Business Cards | Handwritten Notes |
|---|---|---|---|---|
| | | | | |

What did you post today? Blog post, picture, video, or new idea?
_____
_____
_____

What value did you deliver today that sets you apart and makes you different from everyone else?
_____
_____
_____

What is one thing you learned today?
_____
_____
_____

What is one thing you struggled with today?
_____
_____
_____

### COSNOP = Concentrate on Solutions Not on the Problem

What solutions can help you overcome your struggle?
_____
_____
_____

Date _____ / _____ / _____

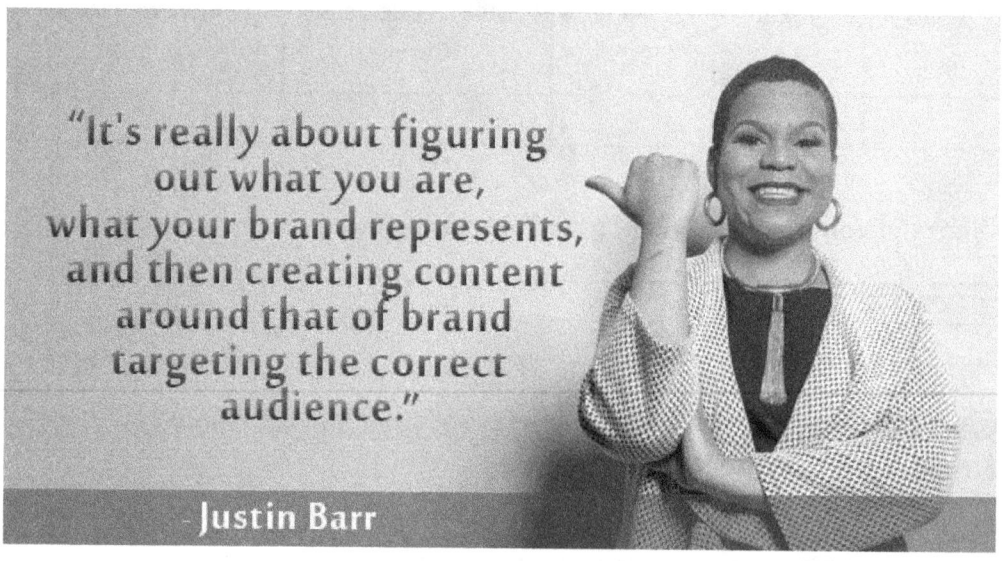

**My Morning Routine**

1)_____
2)_____
3)_____
4)_____
5)_____


**How did you prospect for NEW business today?**

_____
_____
_____
_____
_____

How many calls, texts, emails, mobile business cards and handwritten notes did you send out today?

| Calls | Texts | Emails | Mobile Business Cards | Handwritten Notes |
|---|---|---|---|---|
|  |  |  |  |  |

What did you post today? Blog post, picture, video, or new idea?
_____
_____
_____

What value did you deliver today that sets you apart and makes you different from everyone else?
_____
_____
_____

What is one thing you learned today?
_____
_____
_____

What is one thing you struggled with today?
_____
_____
_____

COSNOP = Concentrate on Solutions Not on the Problem

What solutions can help you overcome your struggle?
_____
_____
_____

Date _____ / _____ / _____

> "If this is your profession and this is your legacy, you have to be relevant. If you're going to be relevant to today's consumer, you have to use social media."
>
> - Jason Frazier

**My Morning Routine**

1) _____
2) _____
3) _____
4) _____
5) _____

**How did you prospect for NEW business today?**

_____
_____
_____
_____
_____

How many calls, texts, emails, mobile business cards and handwritten notes did you send out today?

| Calls | Texts | Emails | Mobile Business Cards | Handwritten Notes |
|-------|-------|--------|----------------------|-------------------|
|       |       |        |                      |                   |

What did you post today? Blog post, picture, video, or new idea?
_____
_____
_____

What value did you deliver today that sets you apart and makes you different from everyone else?
_____
_____
_____

What is one thing you learned today?
_____
_____
_____

What is one thing you struggled with today?
_____
_____
_____

**COSNOP = Concentrate on Solutions Not on the Problem**

What solutions can help you overcome your struggle?
_____
_____
_____

Date _____ /_____ /_____

# WHEN SETTING YOUR GOALS,

**IT'S IMPORTANT TO PAY ATTENTION TO WHAT YOU WANT TO ACHIEVE IN ALL AREAS OF YOUR LIFE.**

-MARKI LEMONS RYHAL

**My Morning Routine**

1)_____
2)_____
3)_____
4)_____
5)_____

**How did you prospect for NEW business today?**

_____
_____
_____
_____
_____

How many calls, texts, emails, mobile business cards and handwritten notes did you send out today?

| Calls | Texts | Emails | Mobile Business Cards | Handwritten Notes |
|-------|-------|--------|----------------------|-------------------|
|       |       |        |                      |                   |

What did you post today? Blog post, picture, video, or new idea?
_____
_____
_____

What value did you deliver today that sets you apart and makes you different from everyone else?
_____
_____
_____

What is one thing you learned today?
_____
_____
_____

What is one thing you struggled with today?
_____
_____
_____

COSNOP = Concentrate on Solutions Not on the Problem

What solutions can help you overcome your struggle?
_____
_____
_____

Date _____ /_____ /_____

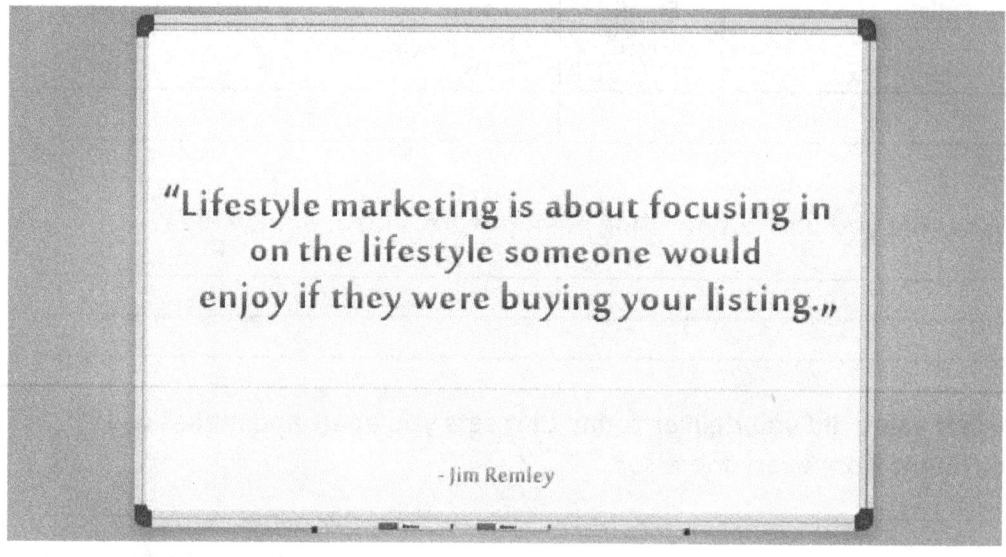

**My Morning Routine**

1)_____
2)_____
3)_____
4)_____
5)_____


**How did you prospect for NEW business today?**

_____
_____
_____
_____
_____

How many calls, texts, emails, mobile business cards and handwritten notes did you send out today?

| Calls | Texts | Emails | Mobile Business Cards | Handwritten Notes |
|---|---|---|---|---|
|  |  |  |  |  |

What did you post today? Blog post, picture, video, or new idea?
_____
_____
_____

What value did you deliver today that sets you apart and makes you different from everyone else?
_____
_____
_____

What is one thing you learned today?
_____
_____
_____

What is one thing you struggled with today?
_____
_____
_____

### COSNOP = Concentrate on Solutions Not on the Problem

What solutions can help you overcome your struggle?
_____
_____
_____

Date _____ / _____ / _____

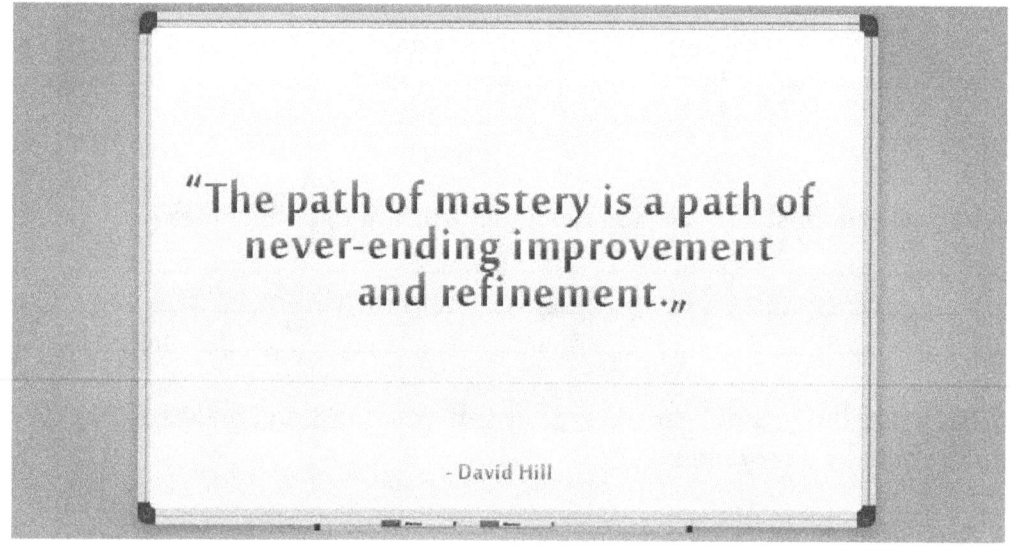

**My Morning Routine**

1)_____
2)_____
3)_____
4)_____
5)_____


**How did you prospect for NEW business today?**

_____
_____
_____
_____
_____

How many calls, texts, emails, mobile business cards and handwritten notes did you send out today?

| Calls | Texts | Emails | Mobile Business Cards | Handwritten Notes |
|-------|-------|--------|-----------------------|-------------------|
|       |       |        |                       |                   |

What did you post today? Blog post, picture, video, or new idea?
_____
_____
_____

What value did you deliver today that sets you apart and makes you different from everyone else?
_____
_____
_____

What is one thing you learned today?
_____
_____
_____

What is one thing you struggled with today?
_____
_____
_____

### COSNOP = Concentrate on Solutions Not on the Problem

What solutions can help you overcome your struggle?
_____
_____
_____

Date _____ / _____ / _____

**My Morning Routine**

1)_____
2)_____
3)_____
4)_____
5)_____


**How did you prospect for NEW business today?**

_____
_____
_____
_____
_____

How many calls, texts, emails, mobile business cards and handwritten notes did you send out today?

| Calls | Texts | Emails | Mobile Business Cards | Handwritten Notes |
|-------|-------|--------|-----------------------|-------------------|
|       |       |        |                       |                   |

What did you post today? Blog post, picture, video, or new idea?
_____
_____
_____

What value did you deliver today that sets you apart and makes you different from everyone else?
_____
_____
_____

What is one thing you learned today?
_____
_____
_____

What is one thing you struggled with today?
_____
_____
_____

**COSNOP = Concentrate on Solutions Not on the Problem**

What solutions can help you overcome your struggle?
_____
_____
_____

Date _____ /_____ /_____

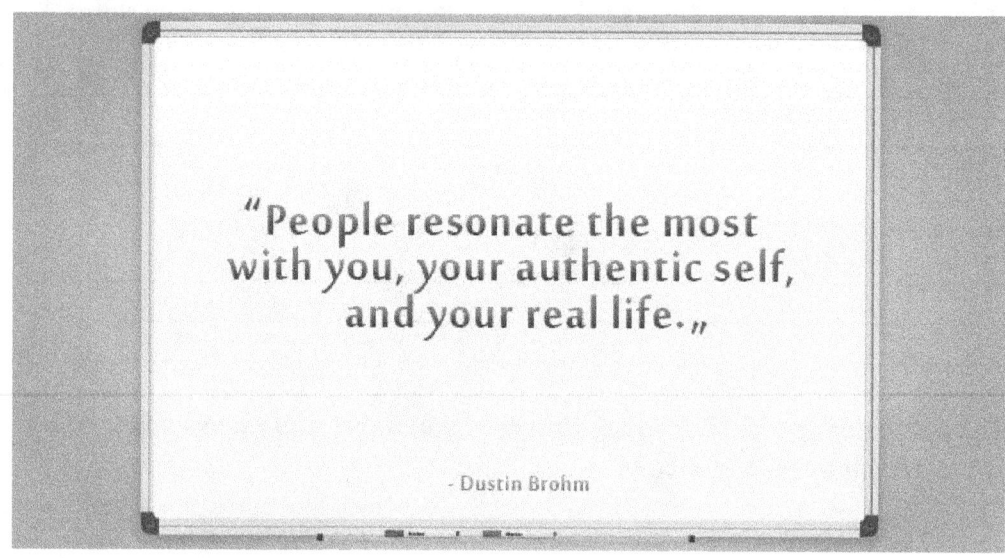

**My Morning Routine**

1)_____
2)_____
3)_____
4)_____
5)_____


**How did you prospect for NEW business today?**

_____
_____
_____
_____
_____

How many calls, texts, emails, mobile business cards and handwritten notes did you send out today?

| Calls | Texts | Emails | Mobile Business Cards | Handwritten Notes |
|-------|-------|--------|----------------------|-------------------|
|       |       |        |                      |                   |

What did you post today? Blog post, picture, video, or new idea?
_____
_____
_____

What value did you deliver today that sets you apart and makes you different from everyone else?
_____
_____
_____

What is one thing you learned today?
_____
_____
_____

What is one thing you struggled with today?
_____
_____
_____

COSNOP = Concentrate on Solutions Not on the Problem

What solutions can help you overcome your struggle?
_____
_____
_____

Date _____ / _____ / _____

# IN ORDER FOR US TO BUILD THAT TRUST WITH TECHNOLOGY, WE'VE GOT { TO MAKE } EYE CONTACT.
## -CHELSEA PEITZ

**My Morning Routine**

1) _____
2) _____
3) _____
4) _____
5) _____


**How did you prospect for NEW business today?**

_____
_____
_____
_____
_____

How many calls, texts, emails, mobile business cards and handwritten notes did you send out today?

| Calls | Texts | Emails | Mobile Business Cards | Handwritten Notes |
|-------|-------|--------|----------------------|-------------------|
|       |       |        |                      |                   |

What did you post today? Blog post, picture, video, or new idea?
_____
_____
_____

What value did you deliver today that sets you apart and makes you different from everyone else?
_____
_____
_____

What is one thing you learned today?
_____
_____
_____

What is one thing you struggled with today?
_____
_____
_____

**COSNOP = Concentrate on Solutions Not on the Problem**

What solutions can help you overcome your struggle?
_____
_____
_____

**Date** _____ / _____ / _____

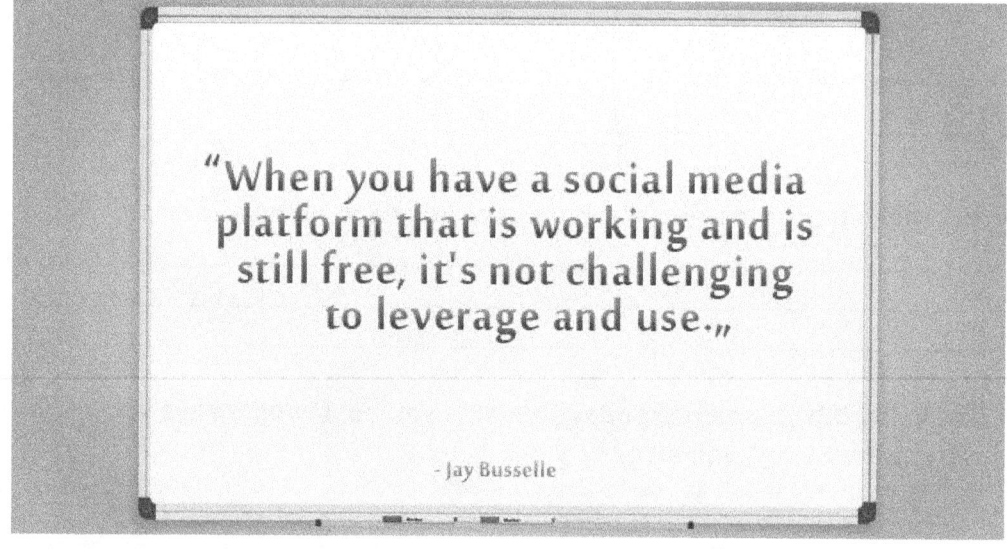

**My Morning Routine**

1)_____
2)_____
3)_____
4)_____
5)_____

**How did you prospect for NEW business today?**

_____
_____
_____
_____
_____

How many calls, texts, emails, mobile business cards and handwritten notes did you send out today?

| Calls | Texts | Emails | Mobile Business Cards | Handwritten Notes |
|-------|-------|--------|----------------------|-------------------|
|       |       |        |                      |                   |

What did you post today? Blog post, picture, video, or new idea?
_____
_____
_____

What value did you deliver today that sets you apart and makes you different from everyone else?
_____
_____
_____

What is one thing you learned today?
_____
_____
_____

What is one thing you struggled with today?
_____
_____
_____

**COSNOP = Concentrate on Solutions Not on the Problem**

What solutions can help you overcome your struggle?
_____
_____
_____

Date _____ /_____ /_____

> "Facebook Ads essentially force your brand and content into the news feeds of the tablets, phones and computers of your target market, instead of a post-and-hope strategy."
>
> - Tristen Sutton

**My Morning Routine**

1) _____
2) _____
3) _____
4) _____
5) _____


**How did you prospect for NEW business today?**

_____
_____
_____
_____
_____

How many calls, texts, emails, mobile business cards and handwritten notes did you send out today?

| Calls | Texts | Emails | Mobile Business Cards | Handwritten Notes |
|-------|-------|--------|----------------------|-------------------|
|       |       |        |                      |                   |

What did you post today? Blog post, picture, video, or new idea?
_____
_____
_____

What value did you deliver today that sets you apart and makes you different from everyone else?
_____
_____
_____

What is one thing you learned today?
_____
_____
_____

What is one thing you struggled with today?
_____
_____
_____

**COSNOP = Concentrate on Solutions Not on the Problem**

What solutions can help you overcome your struggle?
_____
_____
_____

**Date** _____ / _____ / _____

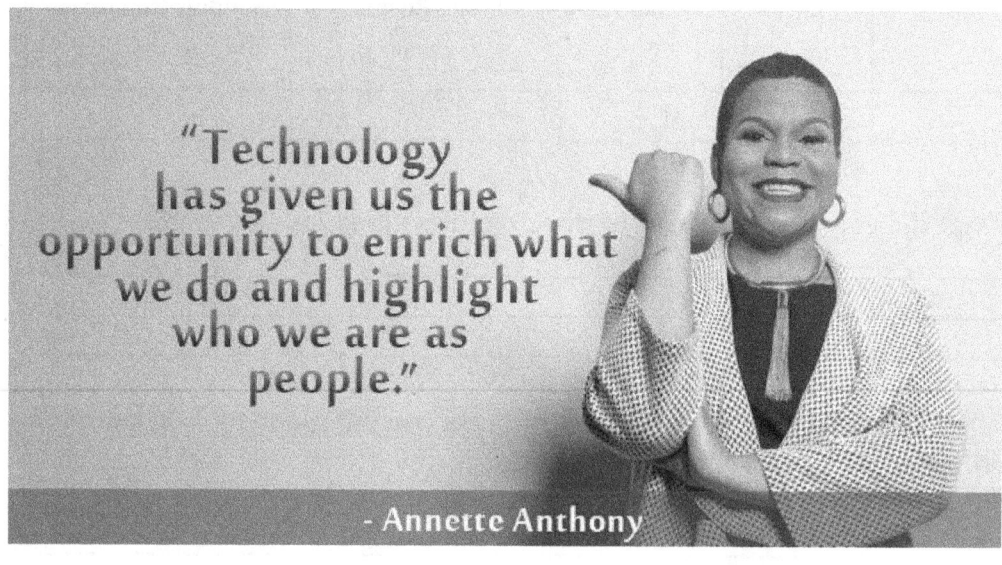

**My Morning Routine**

1)_____
2)_____
3)_____
4)_____
5)_____

**How did you prospect for NEW business today?**

_____
_____
_____
_____
_____

How many calls, texts, emails, mobile business cards and handwritten notes did you send out today?

| Calls | Texts | Emails | Mobile Business Cards | Handwritten Notes |
|-------|-------|--------|-----------------------|-------------------|
|       |       |        |                       |                   |

What did you post today? Blog post, picture, video, or new idea?
_____
_____
_____

What value did you deliver today that sets you apart and makes you different from everyone else?
_____
_____
_____

What is one thing you learned today?
_____
_____
_____

What is one thing you struggled with today?
_____
_____
_____

COSNOP = Concentrate on Solutions Not on the Problem

What solutions can help you overcome your struggle?
_____
_____
_____

Date _____ / _____ / _____

> "If you can get clear on a niche market, and really understand who they are and their interests and behaviors and cater to that niche, 80% of the content should be about what they like."
>
> - Karen Liz Albert

**My Morning Routine**

1) _____
2) _____
3) _____
4) _____
5) _____

**How did you prospect for NEW business today?**

_____
_____
_____
_____
_____

How many calls, texts, emails, mobile business cards and handwritten notes did you send out today?

| Calls | Texts | Emails | Mobile Business Cards | Handwritten Notes |
|---|---|---|---|---|
|  |  |  |  |  |

What did you post today? Blog post, picture, video, or new idea?
___
___
___

What value did you deliver today that sets you apart and makes you different from everyone else?
___
___
___

What is one thing you learned today?
___
___
___

What is one thing you struggled with today?
___
___
___

**COSNOP = Concentrate on Solutions Not on the Problem**

What solutions can help you overcome your struggle?
___
___
___

Date _____ / _____ / _____

> **DON'T BE AFRAID TO ASK FOR THE BUSINESS. IF YOU'RE NOT ACTUALLY PUTTING YOURSELF OUT THERE, YOU'RE WASTING AN OPPORTUNITY.**
> **CANDY MILES-CROCKER**

**My Morning Routine**

1) _____
2) _____
3) _____
4) _____
5) _____

**How did you prospect for NEW business today?**

_____
_____
_____
_____
_____

How many calls, texts, emails, mobile business cards and handwritten notes did you send out today?

| Calls | Texts | Emails | Mobile Business Cards | Handwritten Notes |
|-------|-------|--------|----------------------|-------------------|
|       |       |        |                      |                   |

What did you post today? Blog post, picture, video, or new idea?
_____
_____
_____

What value did you deliver today that sets you apart and makes you different from everyone else?
_____
_____
_____

What is one thing you learned today?
_____
_____
_____

What is one thing you struggled with today?
_____
_____
_____

COSNOP = Concentrate on Solutions Not on the Problem

What solutions can help you overcome your struggle?
_____
_____
_____

Date _____ / _____ / _____

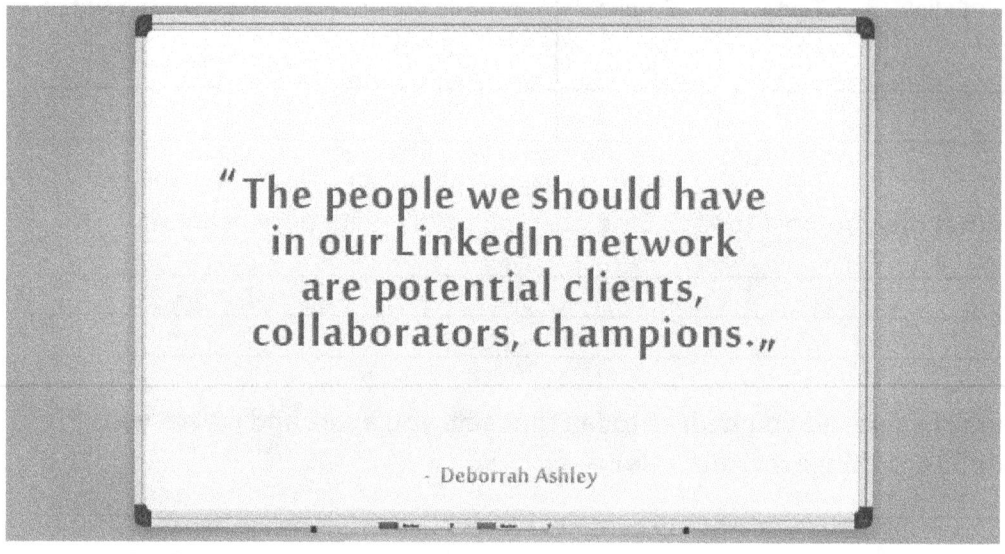

**My Morning Routine**

1)_____
2)_____
3)_____
4)_____
5)_____


**How did you prospect for NEW business today?**

_____
_____
_____
_____
_____

How many calls, texts, emails, mobile business cards and handwritten notes did you send out today?

| Calls | Texts | Emails | Mobile Business Cards | Handwritten Notes |
|---|---|---|---|---|
|   |   |   |   |   |

What did you post today? Blog post, picture, video, or new idea?
_____
_____
_____

What value did you deliver today that sets you apart and makes you different from everyone else?
_____
_____
_____

What is one thing you learned today?
_____
_____
_____

What is one thing you struggled with today?
_____
_____
_____

**COSNOP = Concentrate on Solutions Not on the Problem**

What solutions can help you overcome your struggle?
_____
_____
_____

Date _____ / _____ / _____

> **WHAT TRULY MARKS THE SUCCESS OF YOUR VIDEO CONTENT ISN'T HOW MANY PEOPLE VIEWED.**
> **IT'S ABOUT WHO ACTUALLY ENGAGED WITH IT.**
> **— JAMES REMBERT**

**My Morning Routine**

1) _____
2) _____
3) _____
4) _____
5) _____

**How did you prospect for NEW business today?**

_____
_____
_____
_____
_____

How many calls, texts, emails, mobile business cards and handwritten notes did you send out today?

| Calls | Texts | Emails | Mobile Business Cards | Handwritten Notes |
|-------|-------|--------|----------------------|-------------------|
|       |       |        |                      |                   |

What did you post today? Blog post, picture, video, or new idea?
_____
_____
_____

What value did you deliver today that sets you apart and makes you different from everyone else?
_____
_____
_____

What is one thing you learned today?
_____
_____
_____

What is one thing you struggled with today?
_____
_____
_____

## COSNOP = Concentrate on Solutions Not on the Problem

What solutions can help you overcome your struggle?
_____
_____
_____

Date _____ /_____ /_____

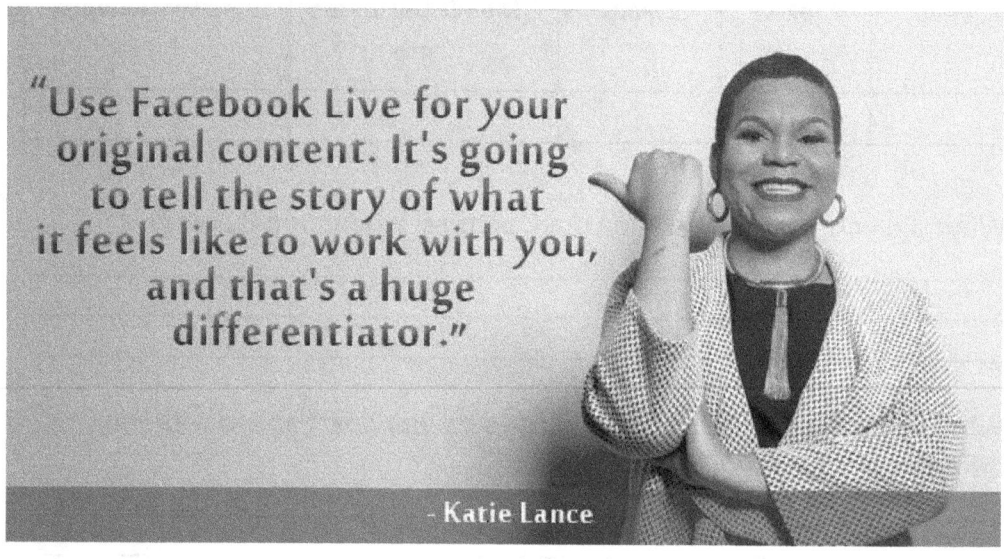

**My Morning Routine**

1)_____
2)_____
3)_____
4)_____
5)_____


**How did you prospect for NEW business today?**

_____
_____
_____
_____
_____

How many calls, texts, emails, mobile business cards and handwritten notes did you send out today?

| Calls | Texts | Emails | Mobile Business Cards | Handwritten Notes |
|-------|-------|--------|----------------------|-------------------|
|       |       |        |                      |                   |

What did you post today? Blog post, picture, video, or new idea?
_____
_____
_____

What value did you deliver today that sets you apart and makes you different from everyone else?
_____
_____
_____

What is one thing you learned today?
_____
_____
_____

What is one thing you struggled with today?
_____
_____
_____

### COSNOP = Concentrate on Solutions Not on the Problem

What solutions can help you overcome your struggle?
_____
_____
_____

Date _____ / _____ / _____

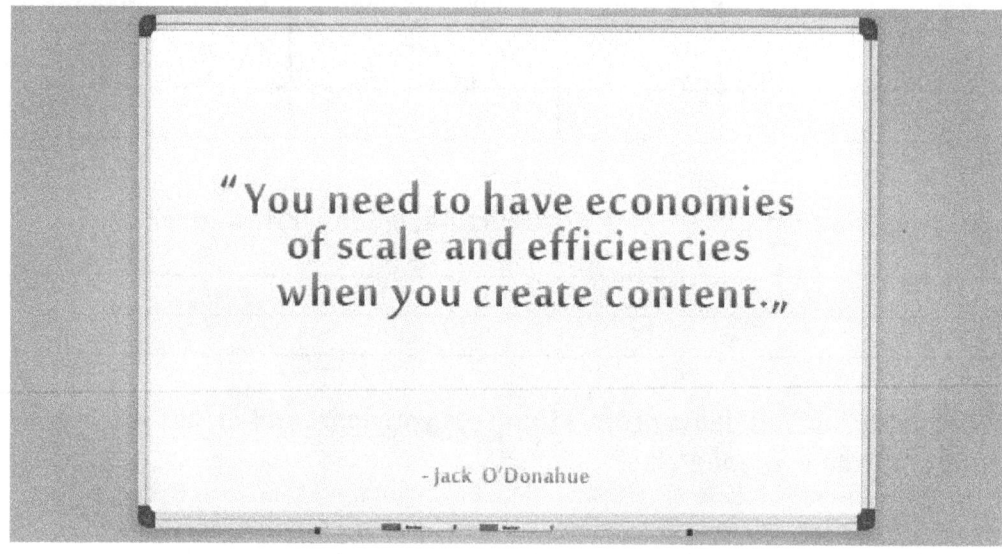

"You need to have economies of scale and efficiencies when you create content."

- Jack O'Donahue

**My Morning Routine**

1)_____
2)_____
3)_____
4)_____
5)_____


**How did you prospect for NEW business today?**

_____
_____
_____
_____
_____

How many calls, texts, emails, mobile business cards and handwritten notes did you send out today?

| Calls | Texts | Emails | Mobile Business Cards | Handwritten Notes |
|---|---|---|---|---|
|  |  |  |  |  |

What did you post today? Blog post, picture, video, or new idea?
_____
_____
_____

What value did you deliver today that sets you apart and makes you different from everyone else?
_____
_____
_____

What is one thing you learned today?
_____
_____
_____

What is one thing you struggled with today?
_____
_____
_____

COSNOP = Concentrate on Solutions Not on the Problem

What solutions can help you overcome your struggle?
_____
_____
_____

Date _____ / _____ / _____

## WE HAVE A 1 IN 50 CHANCE OF CONVERTING PEOPLE WE'VE NEVER MET INTO A CLIENT VERSUS A 1 IN 6 CHANCE OF CONVERTING PEOPLE WE MEET IN PERSON. EVEN WITH ALL THE TECHNOLOGY AND SOCIAL MEDIA, THERE IS MORE VALUE IN MEETING PEOPLE FACE-TO-FACE.
### -MARKI LEMONS-RYHAL

**My Morning Routine**

1) _____
2) _____
3) _____
4) _____
5) _____


**How did you prospect for NEW business today?**

_____
_____
_____
_____
_____

How many calls, texts, emails, mobile business cards and handwritten notes did you send out today?

| Calls | Texts | Emails | Mobile Business Cards | Handwritten Notes |
|-------|-------|--------|----------------------|-------------------|
|       |       |        |                      |                   |

What did you post today? Blog post, picture, video, or new idea?
_____
_____
_____

What value did you deliver today that sets you apart and makes you different from everyone else?
_____
_____
_____

What is one thing you learned today?
_____
_____
_____

What is one thing you struggled with today?
_____
_____
_____

## COSNOP = Concentrate on Solutions Not on the Problem

What solutions can help you overcome your struggle?
_____
_____
_____

**Date** _____ / _____ / _____

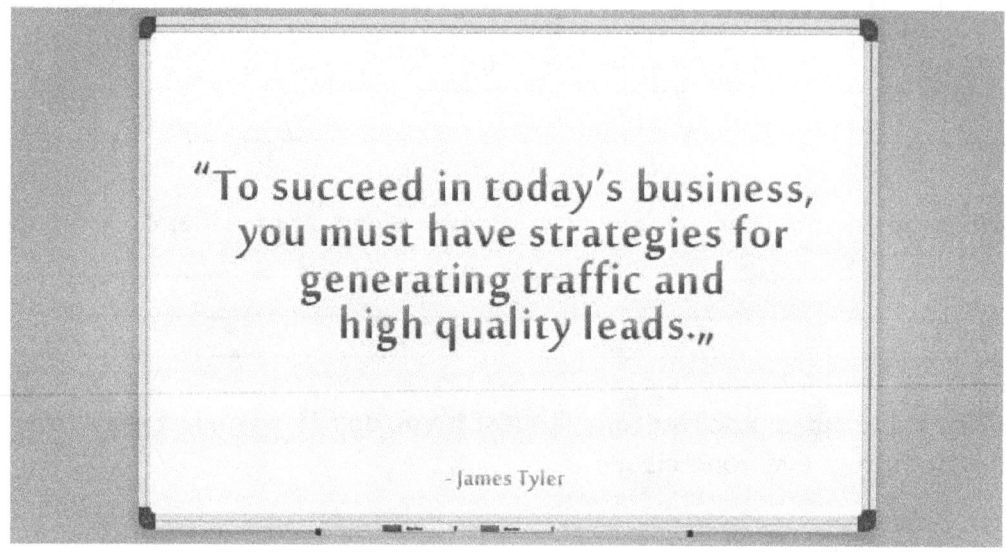

**My Morning Routine**

1)_____
2)_____
3)_____
4)_____
5)_____

**How did you prospect for NEW business today?**

_____
_____
_____
_____
_____

How many calls, texts, emails, mobile business cards and handwritten notes did you send out today?

| Calls | Texts | Emails | Mobile Business Cards | Handwritten Notes |
|-------|-------|--------|-----------------------|-------------------|
|       |       |        |                       |                   |

What did you post today? Blog post, picture, video, or new idea?
_____
_____
_____

What value did you deliver today that sets you apart and makes you different from everyone else?
_____
_____
_____

What is one thing you learned today?
_____
_____
_____

What is one thing you struggled with today?
_____
_____
_____

COSNOP = Concentrate on Solutions Not on the Problem

What solutions can help you overcome your struggle?
_____
_____
_____

Date _____ /_____ /_____

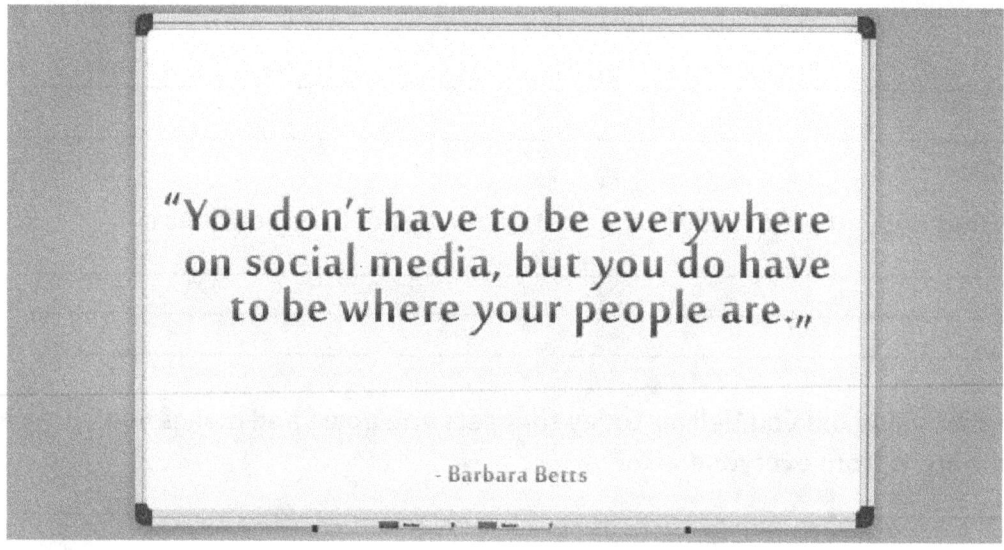

**My Morning Routine**

1)_____
2)_____
3)_____
4)_____
5)_____


**How did you prospect for NEW business today?**

_____
_____
_____
_____
_____

How many calls, texts, emails, mobile business cards and handwritten notes did you send out today?

| Calls | Texts | Emails | Mobile Business Cards | Handwritten Notes |
|-------|-------|--------|----------------------|-------------------|
|       |       |        |                      |                   |

What did you post today? Blog post, picture, video, or new idea?
_____
_____
_____

What value did you deliver today that sets you apart and makes you different from everyone else?
_____
_____
_____

What is one thing you learned today?
_____
_____
_____

What is one thing you struggled with today?
_____
_____
_____

## COSNOP = Concentrate on Solutions Not on the Problem

What solutions can help you overcome your struggle?
_____
_____
_____

Date _____ /_____ / _____

**My Morning Routine**

1)_____
2)_____
3)_____
4)_____
5)_____


**How did you prospect for NEW business today?**

_____
_____
_____
_____
_____

How many calls, texts, emails, mobile business cards and handwritten notes did you send out today?

| Calls | Texts | Emails | Mobile Business Cards | Handwritten Notes |
|-------|-------|--------|----------------------|-------------------|
|       |       |        |                      |                   |

What did you post today? Blog post, picture, video, or new idea?
_____
_____
_____

What value did you deliver today that sets you apart and makes you different from everyone else?
_____
_____
_____

What is one thing you learned today?
_____
_____
_____

What is one thing you struggled with today?
_____
_____
_____

### COSNOP = Concentrate on Solutions Not on the Problem

What solutions can help you overcome your struggle?
_____
_____
_____

Date _____ / _____ / _____

# DON'T BE POOR: PASSING OVER OPPORTUNITIES REPEATEDLY.

-CHAD DURFEE

**My Morning Routine**

1) _____
2) _____
3) _____
4) _____
5) _____

**How did you prospect for NEW business today?**

_____
_____
_____
_____
_____

How many calls, texts, emails, mobile business cards and handwritten notes did you send out today?

| Calls | Texts | Emails | Mobile Business Cards | Handwritten Notes |
|-------|-------|--------|----------------------|-------------------|
|       |       |        |                      |                   |

What did you post today? Blog post, picture, video, or new idea?
_____
_____
_____

What value did you deliver today that sets you apart and makes you different from everyone else?
_____
_____
_____

What is one thing you learned today?
_____
_____
_____

What is one thing you struggled with today?
_____
_____
_____

### COSNOP = Concentrate on Solutions Not on the Problem

What solutions can help you overcome your struggle?
_____
_____
_____

Date \_\_\_\_ / \_\_\_\_ / \_\_\_\_

**My Morning Routine**

1)_____

2)_____

3)_____

4)_____

5)_____

**How did you prospect for NEW business today?**

_____

_____

_____

_____

_____

How many calls, texts, emails, mobile business cards and handwritten notes did you send out today?

| Calls | Texts | Emails | Mobile Business Cards | Handwritten Notes |
|---|---|---|---|---|
|  |  |  |  |  |

What did you post today? Blog post, picture, video, or new idea?
_____
_____
_____

What value did you deliver today that sets you apart and makes you different from everyone else?
_____
_____
_____

What is one thing you learned today?
_____
_____
_____

What is one thing you struggled with today?
_____
_____
_____

COSNOP = Concentrate on Solutions Not on the Problem

What solutions can help you overcome your struggle?
_____
_____
_____

Date _____/_____/_____

> "We believe what we say to ourselves, more than what other people tell us or any other input coming in."
>
> - Anita AC Clinton

**My Morning Routine**

1)_____
2)_____
3)_____
4)_____
5)_____


**How did you prospect for NEW business today?**

_____
_____
_____
_____
_____

How many calls, texts, emails, mobile business cards and handwritten notes did you send out today?

| Calls | Texts | Emails | Mobile Business Cards | Handwritten Notes |
|-------|-------|--------|-----------------------|-------------------|
|       |       |        |                       |                   |

What did you post today? Blog post, picture, video, or new idea?
_____
_____
_____

What value did you deliver today that sets you apart and makes you different from everyone else?
_____
_____
_____

What is one thing you learned today?
_____
_____
_____

What is one thing you struggled with today?
_____
_____
_____

**COSNOP = Concentrate on Solutions Not on the Problem**

What solutions can help you overcome your struggle?
_____
_____
_____

Date _____ /_____ /_____

> "Writing and publishing a book allows you to package your soundbites into a vehicle that can become an asset for you and your business."
>
> - Mitchell Levy

**My Morning Routine**

1)_____
2)_____
3)_____
4)_____
5)_____


**How did you prospect for NEW business today?**

_____
_____
_____
_____
_____

How many calls, texts, emails, mobile business cards and handwritten notes did you send out today?

| Calls | Texts | Emails | Mobile Business Cards | Handwritten Notes |
|---|---|---|---|---|
|  |  |  |  |  |

What did you post today? Blog post, picture, video, or new idea?
___
___
___

What value did you deliver today that sets you apart and makes you different from everyone else?
___
___
___

What is one thing you learned today?
___
___
___

What is one thing you struggled with today?
___
___
___

### COSNOP = Concentrate on Solutions Not on the Problem

What solutions can help you overcome your struggle?
___
___
___

Date ____ / ____ / ____

**My Morning Routine**

1)_____
2)_____
3)_____
4)_____
5)_____


**How did you prospect for NEW business today?**

_____
_____
_____
_____
_____

How many calls, texts, emails, mobile business cards and handwritten notes did you send out today?

| Calls | Texts | Emails | Mobile Business Cards | Handwritten Notes |
|-------|-------|--------|----------------------|-------------------|
|       |       |        |                      |                   |

What did you post today? Blog post, picture, video, or new idea?
_____
_____
_____

What value did you deliver today that sets you apart and makes you different from everyone else?
_____
_____
_____

What is one thing you learned today?
_____
_____
_____

What is one thing you struggled with today?
_____
_____
_____

COSNOP = Concentrate on Solutions Not on the Problem

What solutions can help you overcome your struggle?
_____
_____
_____

Date _____ /_____ / _____

> WE ARE NOW BROADCASTERS
> IN OUR OWN RIGHT.
> THROUGH YOUTUBE, FACEBOOK,
> INSTAGRAM, TWITTER,
> AND LINKEDIN,
> WE CAN CREATE
> QUALITY VIDEO
> CONTENT THAT ALLOWS US
> TO REACH THE MASSES.
> --JEREMIAS "JMAN" MANEIRO

**My Morning Routine**

1)_____
2)_____
3)_____
4)_____
5)_____


**How did you prospect for NEW business today?**

_____
_____
_____
_____
_____

How many calls, texts, emails, mobile business cards and handwritten notes did you send out today?

| Calls | Texts | Emails | Mobile Business Cards | Handwritten Notes |
|-------|-------|--------|----------------------|-------------------|
|       |       |        |                      |                   |

What did you post today? Blog post, picture, video, or new idea?

_____
_____
_____

What value did you deliver today that sets you apart and makes you different from everyone else?

_____
_____
_____

What is one thing you learned today?

_____
_____
_____

What is one thing you struggled with today?

_____
_____
_____

## COSNOP = Concentrate on Solutions Not on the Problem

What solutions can help you overcome your struggle?

_____
_____
_____

CPSIA information can be obtained
at www.ICGtesting.com
Printed in the USA
FSHW010209020720
71262FS